IMAGES THAT SELL:
500 WAYS
TO CREATE
GREAT ADS

White Rock Publishing, Inc., August 1999
Text copyright © 1999 by Luc Dupont
All rights reserved by White Rock Publishing, Inc.

No part of this book may be reproduced in any form or by any means without permission in writing from the publisher.

This book is available at special discounts for bulk purchases by your group or organization for sales promotions, premiums, fundraising and seminars.

For details, contact:
White Rock Publishing, Inc.,
2700 Mont-Joli Street,
Ste-Foy, QC
Canada
G1V 1C8
Phone: (418) 580-9019
Fax: (418) 658-7177
E-mail: whiterockpub@hotmail.com

Cover design by Moisan Marketing
Special thanks to Elliott Moore

Printed in Canada

Legal deposit, 3rd trimester 1999
National Library of Canada

Dupont, Luc, 1964-
Images that Sell: 500 Ways to Create Great Ads.
Bibliography: p.
1. Advertising, 2. Image
3. Visual Communication, 4. Title
ISBN 0-9699834-4-1

LUC DUPONT

IMAGES THAT SELL: 500 WAYS TO CREATE GREAT ADS

WHITE ROCK
PUBLISHING

By the same author:

1001 Advertising Tips, White Rock Publishing, 1999.

Publisher's note

This volume makes use of a large number of advertising images. We are reproducing these images in the spirit of the law that allows for their critical and pedagogical use.

The following ads were taken from *Archive* magazine: p. 31 (top), p. 43 (bottom), p. 46 (bottom), p. 73 (top), p. 82 (above right) p. 83 (bottom), p. 110 (top), p. 113 (top), p. 136 (bottom), p. 138 (bottom), p. 140 (bottom), p. 170, p. 174 (bottom), p. 158 (top), p. 215 (top), p. 218 (top) and p. 257 (below right). To subscribe to *Archive*: USA: American Showcase Inc., 915 Broadway, 14th floor, New York, NY, 10010, Tel. (212) 673-6600; Canada: Keng Seng Enterprises Inc., 315 Traders Blvd. E., Unit 9, Mississauga, ON, L4Z 3E4, Tel. (905) 568-8567.

To Julie

FOREWORD

This is the long-awaited sequel to Luc Dupont's first book, *1001 Advertising Tips*. Since the publication of that first volume, Dupont has analyzed many thousands of advertising images with the purpose of teasing out the particles of thematic significance that advertisers use to stir the fancy of the consuming public.

How does an advertiser use the basic elements of an image to suggest love, the family, or rural life? What are the symbols that are associated with celebration, with culture, or with the idea of the future? Which of the picture's constituent parts convey the idea of wealth, of urbanity, or of material success? Dupont answers these questions for us by presenting 500 of the best ad images ever made.

How do ad images work? And what good are they, anyway? Is their purpose to stimulate artificial needs? Yes, indeed they can have that purpose, because, as professor James B. Twitchell has said, "once we are fed, clothed, and sexually functioning, needs are cultural."

So what these ad images do, then, is to pour meaning into people's lives and into the life of society. And central to this meaning is the all-important sense of belonging to a specific social group. Let us be frank about this: we do not really need the objects we covet and buy; and yet we do feel something very much like a need for their symbolic value. These days, when you are 35 years old, and you're trying to establish yourself in a prominent and successful business milieu, you actually need a Mont Blanc fountain-pen, a Hugo Boss shirt, and a BMW automobile. And when you're a teenager, and the one thing you want most in the world is to be part of your school's "in" group, you need Nike shoes, Gap clothes, and a Sony Diskman.

Per capita, North America spends twice as much on advertising as Europe does: in the U.S., close to $400 for every man, woman, and child are invested in advertising each year; in France, the figure is $160. The purpose of this investment is the creation and building up of brand names.

And it would seem furthermore that these investments are successful. As Juliet Schor has pointed out, research shows that the average North-American possesses four times as many objects as does the average European.

In any case, the art of persuasion seems to be working well. What are best-known luxury brand-names in the western world? Armani, Laura Ashley, Bang & Olufsen, Pierre Cardin, Cartier, Chanel, Chivas Regal: in other words, the leading image producers! Are these not the brands that dominate our dream and desires?

Image as stereotype James B. Twitchell has stated: "We live through things. We create ourselves through things. And we change ourselves by changing our things. We often depend on such material things for meaning." Sombre news? Perhaps, but how extremely human!

Astute advertisers play upon this fundamental need for meaning. Their images mold and shape meaning, breathe meaning into objects. They stimulate the desire for objects in people who hope to become, through acquisition, the person they feel themselves to be.

Increasingly, the possession of things is becoming the defining attribute of being. The greatest adversity, the greatest poverty, is to find oneself unable to flaunt the objects that are already possessed by most people in our social group.

Ad images are the seat of powerful symbols whose meaning gets transferred to certain objects, specifically those commodities with which they are associated in the ad. One wears Obsession perfume to acquire the power to seduce the beautiful models in the ad image; one drives the New Beetle as in a newly acquired youth evoked by the colors of the ad posters; by conspicuously opening one's ThinkPad, one repeats a spectacle stage-managed by the ads in the business magazines. Nudity and luxury: the limited repertory is simplicity itself. Dupont shows all this very profoundly: advertisers, in order to evoke feelings, situations, and associations, continually make use of the same stereotypes. In fact, Dupont shows us how mass communications work.

It is true that in able hands, the image is an instrument of near-magical persuasive powers. Contemporary advertising could not exist without it. This is what Dupont reveals in his far-reaching effort to simplify and explain this world of illusions, and to render it accessible to the layman.

* * *

Image advertising is so successful that the 10% of the world's population most exposed to ads (a demographic of which we are part) consumes 90% of the world's resources. To have the Luc Dupont's "dictionary" will allow each of us better to understand how the persuasive message behaves, and if need be, to caution us against the mirages of what Vance Packard called "hidden persuasion".

Claude Cossette
Professor of Advertising
Founder of Cossette Communication-Marketing

TABLE OF CONTENTS

	Foreword	7
	Introduction	13
1	America	17
2	Animals	23
3	Babies	53
4	The Body	63
5	Brand Names	117
6	Celebrities	119
7	Children	125
8	The City	131
9	The Countryside	135
10	Culture	141
11	Death	147
12	The Earth	151
13	The Elderly	157
14	Exoticism	161
15	The Family	175
16	Festivities	179
17	Fictitious Characters	181

18	The Future and Outer Space	183
19	Graphic Creativity	187
20	The House	193
21	Institutional Characters	197
22	Legendary Characters	199
23	Love	203
24	Man	217
25	The Past	221
26	Religion	227
27	Sexuality	231
28	Social Problems	237
29	Sport	243
30	Time	247
31	Wealth	251
32	Woman	259
33	Young People	265
	Conclusion	267
	Bibliography	269

INTRODUCTION

In the following pages, I propose to analyse some of the most efficient advertising images ever produced. My purpose: to show you how to base your ad campaigns on images that sell.

You will discover:

- How people react to advertising images
- Why image choice is so important in advertising
- Which images attract the most attention
- Which images are most readily memorized
- Which images are most favored
- Which images are most disliked
- Which images sell

The principles that I will be establishing in this book hold true for nearly all types of product and service, whether you are selling a car, a soft drink, a computer, a religion, or a political candidate.

You will find this book's ideas to apply to all media that contain images, especially magazines, billboards, daily and weekly newspapers, television, subway and bus ads, catalogs, and the telephone-book yellow pages.

To facilitate reading, each chapter will deal succinctly with a specific theme, such as that of femininity or of the city, for example. Each chapter will also include commentary on a great many images, for a total of over 500 color ads. With the help of these concrete examples, I intend to examine in a practical manner the ways in which you can influence and motivate consumers with images.

Why are my advertising examples all based upon image-based communication? Because, as Paul Almasy has pointed out, pictorial ads today are memorized by forty-one percent more readers than are text ads. In fact, in a world where we are potentially exposed to 3,000 advertising messages per day, the Starch research firm has discovered that advertising texts are read, on average, by only nine percent of readers. This means that it is absolutely illusory to imagine that you can effectively persuade consumers without recourse to the power of the image.

The use of images presents a great advantage. A picture plays on the sentiments, and it can communicate a complex message in the twinkling of an eye. It does this without even requiring that the ad be read and without demanding the complicated effort of reflection. For example:

- the freshness of a cool glass of beer can be evoked by associating it with a piece of ice or with a cascading waterfall;
- the braking power of a car can be expressed by associating it with a parachute;
- the lightness of a suitcase can be represented by the picture of a feather;
- the power of a brand of gasoline is suggested by the image of a black horse at full gallop.

In order to persuade the consumer to buy your product, you must learn to decipher the language of images.

Of course, consumers will never admit that their choice of any product has been influenced by images. Instead, people, will invariably claim that they base their purchases solely upon objective data. In fact, if you ask them: "Are you influenced by advertising?", most people will confidently tell you that advertising and marketing simply do not work. These people will claim that they are capable of determining quality and of distinguishing between products on purely objective grounds, without recourse to advertising messages. This is false.

Take the case of Sanyo and RCA. Recently, researchers pasted a Sanyo label on an appliance manufactured by RCA, then asked 900 people to compare its performance with that of the very same product presented under the original RCA label. Seventy percent of these people claimed that the Sanyo product was clearly superior. Nevertheless, in every instance, the two appliances, both manufactured by RCA, were identical.

Then there is the case of the Michelin tire company. Some time ago, this company made a major change in its ads by introducing charming pictures of babies shown seated in their tires. Interestingly, since the appearance of these sweet infants in their ads, Michelin sales in North America have shot up dramatically in a way that previous campaigns had never been able to achieve. And yet, the tires are exactly the same as they always were!

Similarly, it was sufficient for the Marlboro cigarette company to place images of wranglers and horses into its ads for its sales to surpass those of any other cigarette manufacturer world-wide.

In other words, when consumers spend money, they purchase not only a product, but, along with that product, entire complexes of images and emotions. These images and emotions can be associated with babies, animals, colors, shapes, brand names, and an infinite variety of other deeply meaningful symbols.

The images contained in this book, however different they may be from each other, all share one outstanding strength: they attract the consumer's attention, and they use emotion to communicate particular aspects of a product. These images position their products in consumers' minds while delivering a message — all in a fraction of a second.

1

AMERICA

For economic, cultural, and historical reasons, it can often be very profitable to draw liberally upon the power of the American myth. In advertising, as in cinema and elsewhere, America is a powerful symbol of abundance and of the promised land. Symbols of America are therefore extremely useful in reaching out to readers and in ensuring their identification with your product. That this should hold true not only in America, but throughout the world, gives some degree of insight into the astonishing power of the American myth.

A good many images testify to the permanence of U.S. culture and its symbols. Strong sentiment is of course associated with the Stars and Stripes, but this is also true of the Statue of Liberty, the American eagle, the Declaration of Independence, and the White House.

Furthermore, the American myth is intimately associated with the Far West and with the cinematic tradition of the western adventure story. The western image is one of endurance, hope, and a stalwart individualism.

If you want to call up associations with the West in the mind of your reader, do not hesitate to refer to the time-tested images of cowboys, American Indians, and the desert. Obviously, what counts here is not so much the arid landscape itself, but rather the image that this geographical reality can call up in the mind of your prospective customer: specifically, that of the harsh and demanding circumstances that test a man's courage.

See also: the city

Top:

The American flag is still the primary symbol of American patriotism. It can sell nearly anything, from clothing and cigarettes to perfume and automobiles.

Bottom:

Because America is such a powerful symbol of vitality and abundance, an image showing the Statue of Liberty in a predicament is very likely to surprise your readers, and thereby attract their attention.

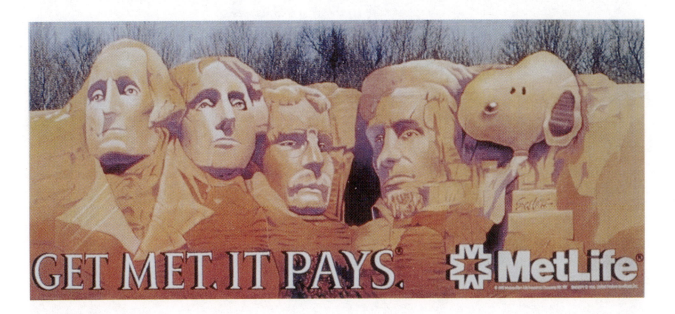

RUSS TROLL A President for the ages. For all ages.

He is, of course, the Ideal Candidate. Leaning neither to the left nor to the right, Russ Troll brings to his candidacy a popularity that has captivated the nation.

Only he could live up to his slogan "What this country needs is some good luck," for they do say that rubbing a Russ Troll's hair can bring good luck.

His platform is one upon which everyone can agree: a country free of drugs, with work opportunities for everyone, and stronger family ties.

Once elected, with his smiling face firmly in place on Mount Russmore, he will indeed be a President for the ages.

Show your support for this candidate who, though short in size, is big of heart. Wear his campaign button, flaunt his bumper sticker, read about him in the "Troll Times" and proudly display his posters.

You'll find them all at any Russ Troll Campaign Headquarters. For the one nearest you, call this
**TROLL-FREE NUMBER:
1-800-343-7877.**

© 1992 Russ Berrie and Company, Inc.

When you modify a familiar image, you create what amounts to a visual hook. This can be quite handily done with objects, animals, or persons.

By using pictures of politicians, you impart a certain notoriety to your ad. For example, inserting an image of Ronald Reagan into an ad can greatly magnify the ad's ability to grab readers' attention.

During the beginning of his presidential mandate, Bill Clinton habitually ended his morning jog by stopping at McDonald's and enjoying a cup of coffee and a chat with other customers. His morning visit brought the hamburger chain considerable visibility.

An emotionally-based American mythology is rooted in images of the cowboy and the Far West. The West is synonymous with endurance and conquest.

When advertising expert Leo Burnett was given the budget for Marlboro cigarettes in 1954, the brand had only a small share of the market. Smokers found the filter tip effeminate. So Burnett decided to position them as cigarettes for men. To get across this new image, he used the picture of a cowboy and galloping wild horses to stress masculinity. No woman ever appeared in Marlboro's print advertising or television commercials. Marlboro quickly became the leader in sales, a position it has never relinquished.

2

ANIMALS

In the western-European and North-American cultural tradition, the reassuring presence of animals starts from early childhood. For this reason, animals make excellent symbols and "spokespersons".

As advertisers will tell you, an animal inserted into your visual constitutes a sure-fire way of attracting the public's attention. According to John Caples, animal photos, in terms of efficiency, come just after photos of weddings and babies. One important fact to keep in mind is that, in advertising, the animal category includes all manner of beasts as well as insects, fish, and birds.

Interestingly enough, advertising research indicates that men prefer photographs of dogs, while women will invariably pay more attention to photos of cats and horses. But make no mistake: it is not because your photograph attracts attention that it will necessarily make someone buy your product. For that to happen, you will have to establish a bond between your chosen animal, your particular concept, and your product.

Who can possibly be unaware of the fact that the elephant has a long memory, that the tortoise is slow, and that the grasshopper would rather have fun? If a species looks fierce, it will make a good war symbol. If another looks sweet and cuddly, it will naturally express the qualities of childhood. When all is said and done, ads are never really what they seem to be: rather, they are tools to help you express values and states of mind.

In advertising, the dog is indispensable to the representation of the happy family. According to John Caples, animal photos, in terms of efficiency, come just after photos of weddings and babies.

Just like all other animals, the dog can be made the object of a great many visual gags. According to your particular needs, go ahead and reshape its body, give it a human appearance, show it in a variety of different situations.

Top:

In order to produce a good shock effect, do not hesitate to impart canine attributes to a cat. For the sake of creativity, you can do the same with other animals as well. For example, go ahead and dress up a zebra with a cow's spots or an elephant with a giraffe's neck.

Bottom:

The black cat is in a class by itself. Suggestive of slinky movement and seductive beauty, it can represent femininity and wealth. It is ideal for advertising products of refinement and luxury.

The characteristic features of the horse provide a full range of dynamic metaphors that you can use to evoke both speed and vigor.

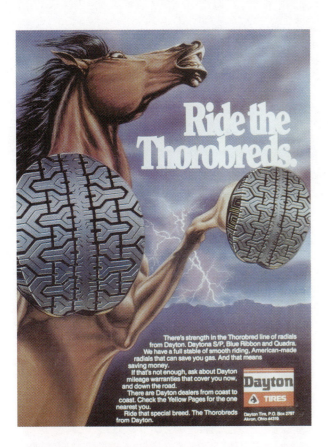

If you want to have your ad exemplify refinement and good taste, consider using pictures of riding-horses and scenes from polo games.

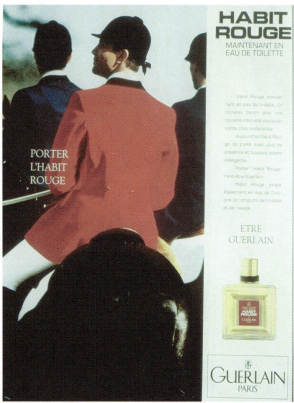

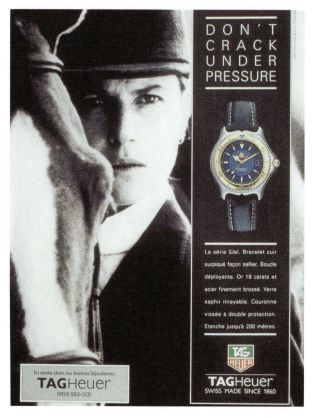

Top:

The cow is a real cult-object in advertising. With its slow, contented demeanor and its gentle face, the cow has a congenial and sweetly comical appearance. Use it for all sorts of whimsical purposes.

Bottom:

You can easily suggest the idea of virile strength and vigor with the bull. Like the goat, the buffalo, and the rhinoceros, this animal symbolizes raw power. Its horns alone are suggestive of robust energy, as are the horns of all horned animals.

The wolf exemplifies strength and cunning. It also inspires dread. Its characteristic fierceness is unleashed upon animals less strong than itself.

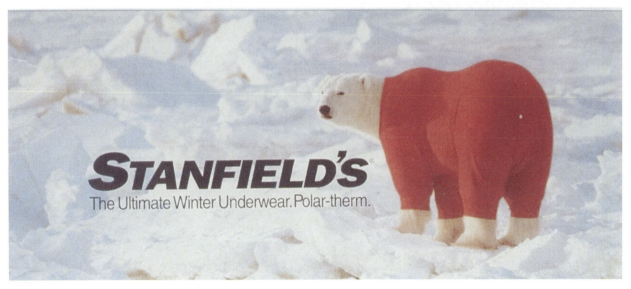

Top:

In general, the bear is a symbol of the warrior.

Bottom:

Like the penguin, the polar bear suggests a frigid climate.

The piglet evokes the idea of thrift and of economical good sense. But by insisting upon its corkscrew tail, its muzzle, and the absurd wings which it is sometimes made to wear, you can turn it into a very amusing animal.

The sheep suggests slumber, that is, "counting sheep". It is also the perfect symbol for the victim led to the slaughterhouse.

The rabbit is a small and delicate animal. It is closely associated with both carrots and magic. According to some tales and legends, the rabbit, in addition to being exceptionally swift, is endowed with an extraordinary sense of sight. Being also particularly fertile, it also strongly suggests good luck. In the above photograph, one reads, in French, "Unkillable".

Top:

The tortoise is associated with sluggishness. Therefore, if you wish to surprise your readers, give this animal a tail-fin in order to suggest speed.

Bottom:

The giraffe is characterized by its long neck and legs. One associates it both with slow movement and outlandish height.

Top:

The lion is the traditional king of animals. The very incarnation of power, of fierceness, and of courage, the lion is also supremely confident. In circuses, it is into the mouth of the lion that the lion-tamer places his head, as if to defy its power.

Bottom:

The camel, as a mount used for desert crossings, suggests endurance and adventure.

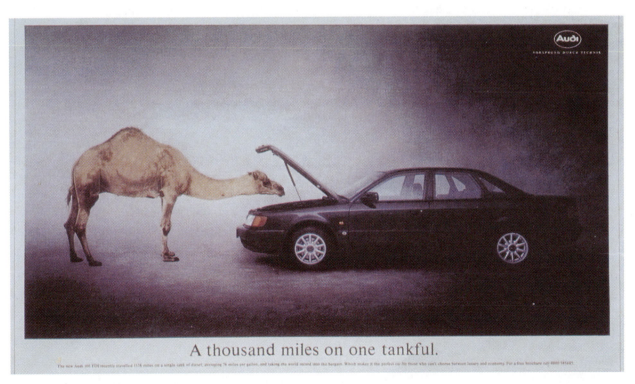

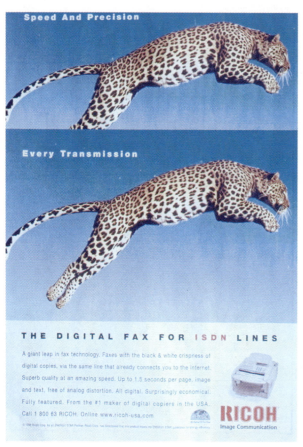

The tiger, the panther, and the leopard, either leaping or striking out with a massive paw, evoke power and ferocity. Beautiful, cruel, and quick, these great cats simultaneously fascinate and terrify.

The gaping muzzle of the crocodile gives it a voracious appearance. Associate it with food and with teeth. Above, an ad for dentists.

Top:

The monkey is well known for its agility, its gift of imitation, and its buffoonery. Its resemblance to human beings serves to illustrate evolution with humor. Its taste for bananas is legendary.

Bottom:

The gorilla is an ungainly, lumbering animal whose imposing physique inspires respect.

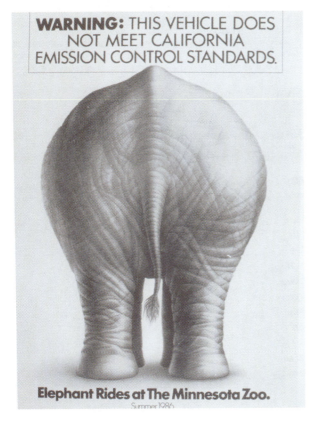

The elephant symbolizes force, great weight, and obstinacy. Furthermore, the elephant is said to possess a prodigious memory.

The snake is one of the most feared of all animals. According to the biblical story of creation, God created the snake as the antagonist of man. In the context of advertising, the snake is a sign of danger. Along with the hairy spider, it is the animal that people most scorn.

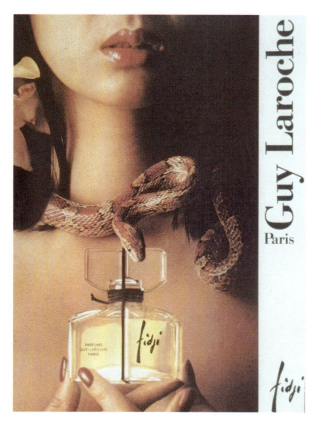

The snake can sometimes be used as a blatant phallic symbol.

In this example, the head of the snake, much like an arrow, pulls the reader's gaze towards the product.

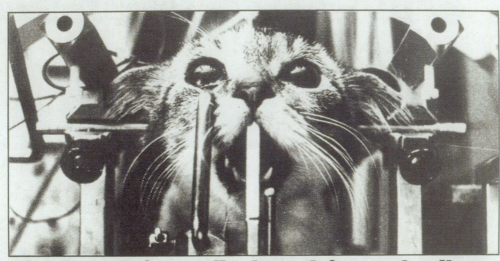

Images of violence based on the depiction of animals are surprising. They generally shock the reader.

Make your prospective customer shudder by showing him a bug in less than perfect condition.

Top: use the snail to represent slow movement.
Bottom: suggest persistent, tenacious activity with the ant. Industrious and well-organized, the ant, like the squirrel, symbolizes prudence and foresight.

The butterfly should be used in images suggestive of levity and grace.

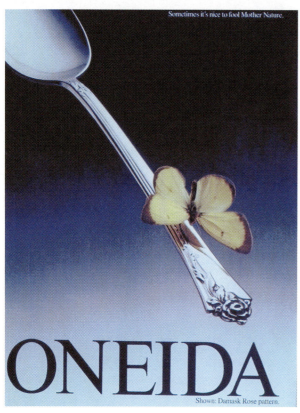

Many varieties of fish can be seen in ads. They are depicted either for their physical particularities, their behavior, or for their value as a source of nutrition. The goldfish, however, remains the undisputed star.

If you are willing to take some extra time, you can create strong, creative ads using images of fish.

In the world of business, as in that of advertising, danger is symbolized by the shark.

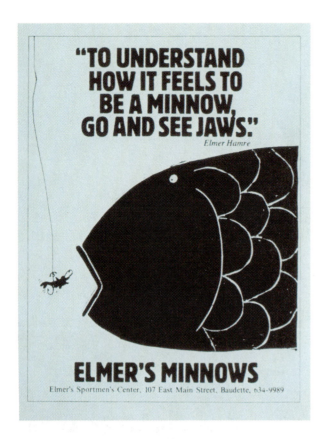
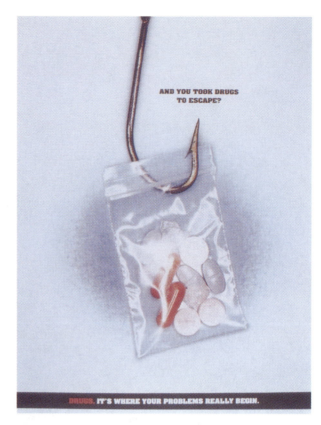

Top:

The hook suggests naiveté. To be hooked is to be trapped.

Bottom:

The image of a big fish in the process of devouring a smaller one gives apt expression to the idea of domination.

The frog is a curious-looking little creature. The phases of the frog's development have spawned allegories of permutation and innovation. In tales, a young girl's kiss transforms the frog into a prince, and the contemptible is made magnificent.

Top:

Birds offer opportunities for many vivid illustrations, the best-known being those of the take-off and the V-shaped flight formation.

Bottom:

Appearing on several national flags, the eagle stands for invincible might. It is considered to be the most majestic of birds.

The ostrich, with its head buried in the sand, has long symbolized the desire to ignore danger or escape reality.

3

BABIES

Many advertisers use pictures of babies to illustrate their ads. This is often an excellent idea. Advertising research indicates that photos of babies attract almost twice as much attention as any other type of illustration.

One subject that works extremely well is the new-born baby. Extol its innocence. Show the baby at the center of its parents' attention, bringing love and reconciliation into their lives.

Devote special attention to objects associated with early childhood. When possible, introduce stuffed animals, toy blocks, diapers, safety pins, pacifier, bottle, high-chair, and stroller.

At the same time, make use of images of the baby himself. In advertising, the various ways of using pictures of the body are a constant concern, and baby is certainly no exception to this rule.

Babies are of immense importance in the advertising image. Their presence in a picture arouses deep emotion and constitutes a strong impetus for the reader to identify simultaneously with the situation described and with the product. For that reason, the baby is the star of any ad.

See also: family and children

To make your images work at peak efficiency, I would advise either that you portray the new-born baby or that you make use of the eagerness and anxiety associated with the anticipation of birth. For this, use conspicuous, noteworthy symbols: a baby still within its mother's womb, a pregnant woman, or a stork.

In your images, extol the new-born baby's innocence and natural spontaneity. Show babies in the care of mothers, fathers, or grandparents.

Now more than at any time in the past, it is to the advertiser's advantage to show babies in their fathers' care. According to Cossette and Déry, this subject reveals the deep-seated maternal instinct that men naturally share with women.

Ads that show more than one baby are generally very effective. Babies are peerless communicators of abstract ideas. The more the message seems complicated and hard to communicate, the more one will find babies to be valuable messengers.

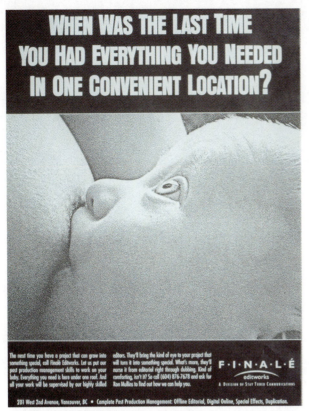

Be sure to make full use of the positive connotations associated with the idea of the child's development, or his desire to walk, to suckle, or to eat.

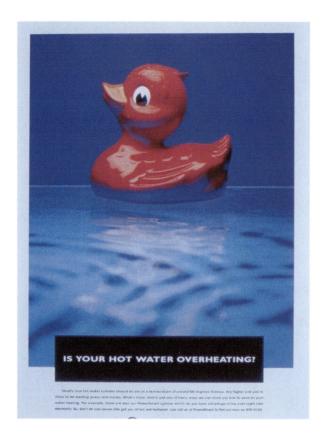

Pay special attention to objects associated with early childhood. The new-born receives constant care and attention. The presence of this attention is reflected in the various objects that are found around the baby.

Likewise, these same objects can be used to illustrate such concepts as independent thinking or simplicity.

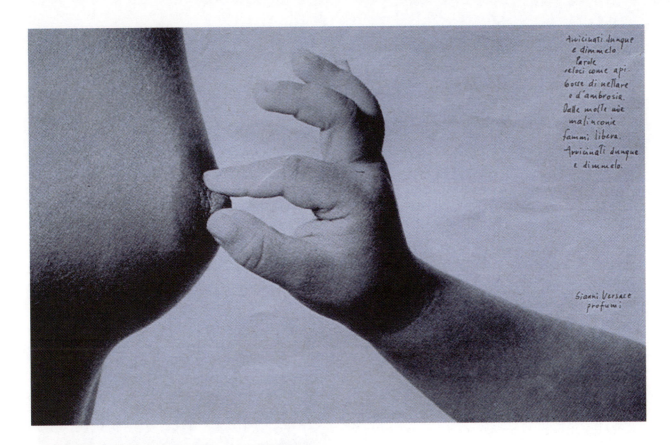

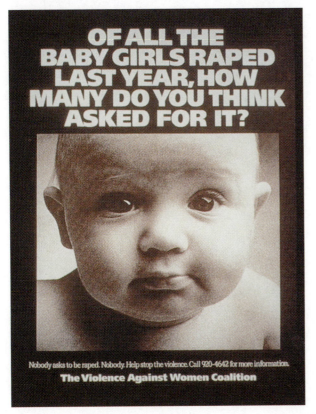

Top:

The hand that reaches out for contact with the world is a powerful advertising tool. If you show a baby reaching out to an adult, you suggest the appeal for help and love.

Bottom:

Make creative use of images of the baby himself. Show his tiny size or reveal his face in close-ups.

Nude babies are a good way to win the attention of your potential clients.

Some of the baby's facial expressions will attract the attention of your readers, among them: smiling and crying, fear and surprise.

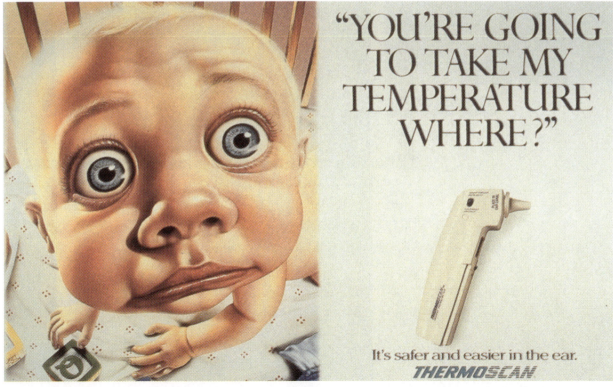

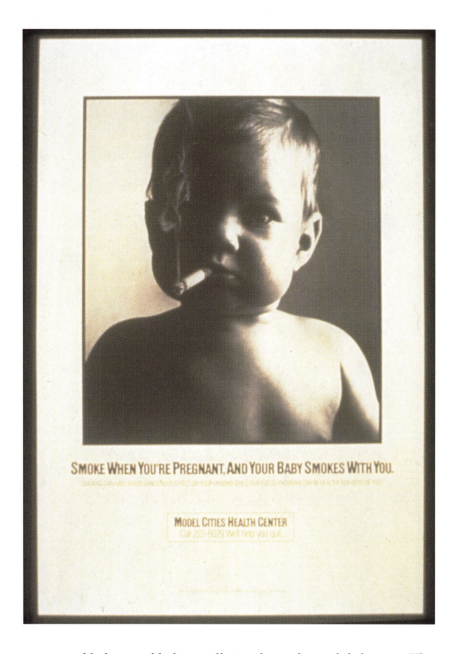

Avoid depicting mistreated babies and babies suffering from physical deformity. The world of early childhood is entirely comprised of softness, lightness, and bliss. It is an idealized time of life, during which misfortune need not play a role.

In some cases, by having your babies behave as if they were adults, you may inspire humor and even cause your reader to stop and think.

4

THE BODY

Since the advertising image is based on the symbolic use of visual material, readers generally know, through the force of a long acculturation, how to interpret and understand the various illustrations of the human body that appear in ads.

Generally, the body in advertising corresponds to an invariable set of canons: the advertising body is a young and healthy body, tall, slender, and strong.

When you work with illustrations of the body, pay close attention to the face. The expression of the face will always exert a strong influence on the emotions of those persons to whom you are eager to communicate your message. According to academic researchers, the face counts for over fifty-five percent of all perceived impressions during any human interaction. In comparison, verbal content counts for no more than seven percent!

Several studies have confirmed the fact that ad images showing beautiful people significantly determine the public's perception of the advertised product.

Research also shows that we naturally presume attractive persons to possess talent, honesty and intelligence. In comparison to less attractive persons, they are perceived to be more outgoing and more sexually fulfilled.

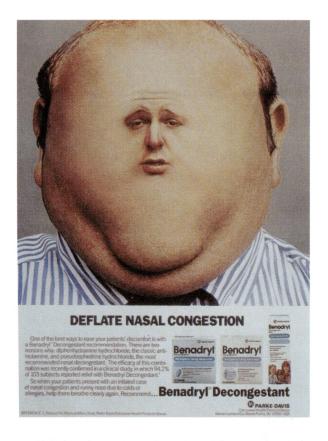

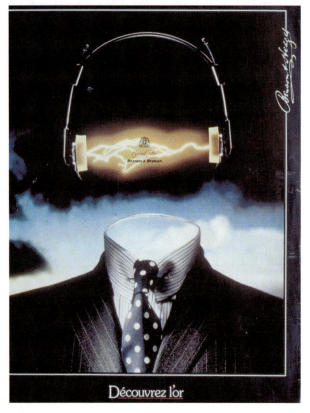

You can modify the appearance of the head in many ways. In more extreme cases, you may wish to go so far as to separate it from the rest of the body, isolate it or modify its shape.

Top:

In images of women, long hair can always be used for its provocative and erotic quality.

Bottom:

To increase the seductive power of your images, show women in the process of raising their hair. By allowing the hair to fall over the shoulders, you can suggest seduction and intimacy.

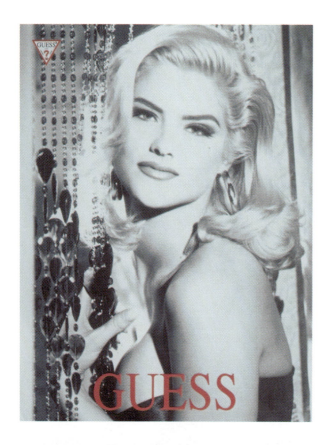

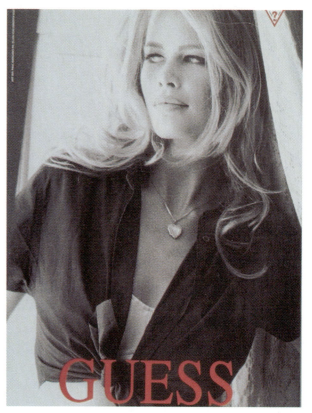

The hair-color of your models is an important aspect of your ads.

Top:

Blond women tend to evoke an aura of dependence and a need for protection. Blond hair also carries an extremely strong sexual connotation.

Bottom:

Brunettes appear to be independent. They are also associated with the family and security. According to Baker, brunettes are typically associated with the quality of refinement.

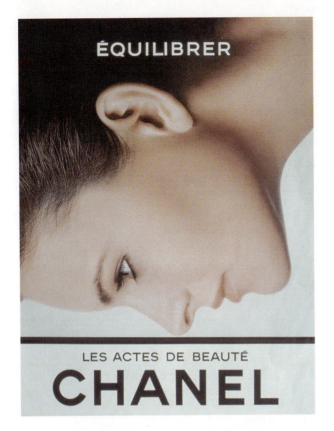

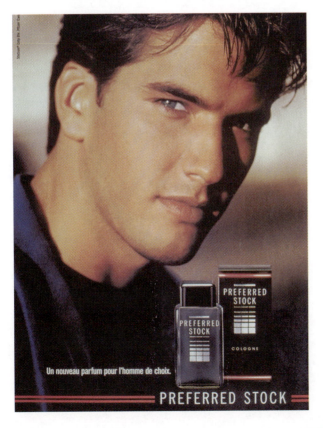

In your images, show beautiful faces, frozen and artificial, with the clean lines that immediately suggest the model or actor. Choose young, attractive women with flawless skin. And in men, the bony face and the square, heavy jaw always assure an aggressive look.

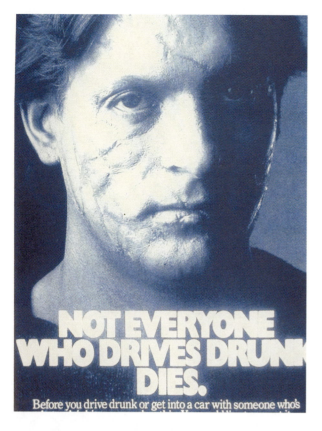
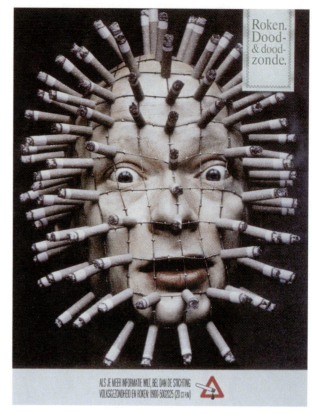

Top:

Since we are all conditioned to see beauty, you can attract immediate attention and create surprise with modified or even disfigured facial lines.

Bottom:

Avoid wrinkles and grey hair, and be careful with facial hair. Beards are associated with thinkers, warriors, and artists. A clean-shaven man will always appear younger and friendlier.

Show people with a tanned complexion. The suntan is synonymous with holidays, wealth and fulfilment.

However, it should be pointed out that the models that appear in ads these days seem to be less tanned than they once were. Of course, this is not an accident. Faced with an important rise in skin cancer and with the explicit warnings of dermatologists, advertisers have begun to adapt the images of their ads.

Two ads created by the French tanning-lotion firm Bain de Soleil, appearing ten years apart, illustrate this change.

Top:

This model's skin is very dark. The ad appeared at the beginning of the 1980's.

Bottom:

The same advertiser here prefers to use a model whose complexion is lighter. The ad is from the 1990's.

Always try to put an ethnically and culturally diverse group into the picture. With multi-ethnic gatherings, you suggest the idea of brotherhood and of universality. In this way, it is likely that you will simultaneously promote your readers' identification with your ad. One way to vary this idea is by showing models of different age groups, both young and old, instead of different ethnic groups.

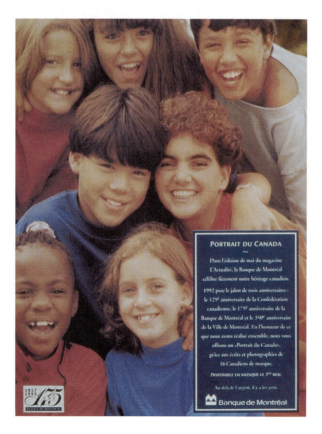

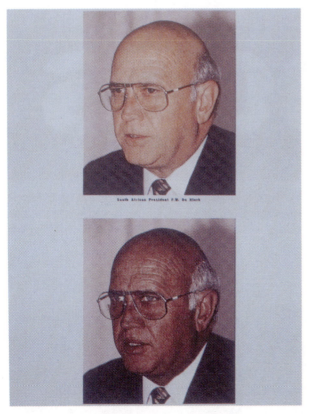

Top:

In this image, the white-black contrast is reinforced by the political and social dimension of the decor: an inexplicably cheerful-looking black man is surrounded by members of the Ku Klux Klan.

Bottom:

In an anti-racist advertising campaign, former South-African president de Klerk's skin color has been changed from white to black. This image was used to launch an anti-apartheid social message. The objective here is not only to proclaim anyone's right to be different, but also the freedom of all to live together in brotherhood.

In advertising, the gaze is a powerful tool for reflecting a wide range of emotions, such as surprise, distress, and seduction.

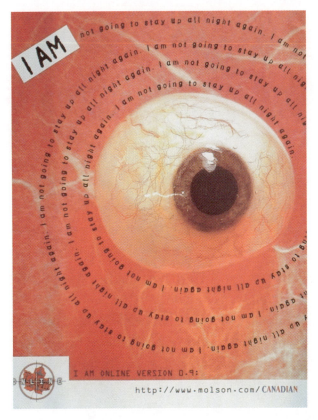

To surprise and attract your reader, exaggerate the natural lines of the eye. For example, use make-up or artificial lashes to "enlarge" the eyes of your models. Eyes can be made to flash dramatically.

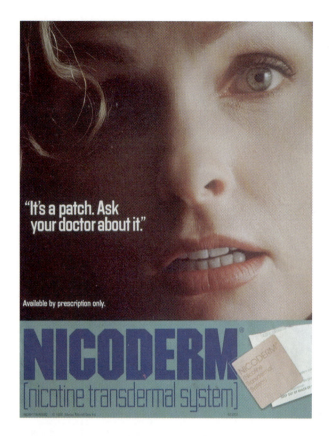
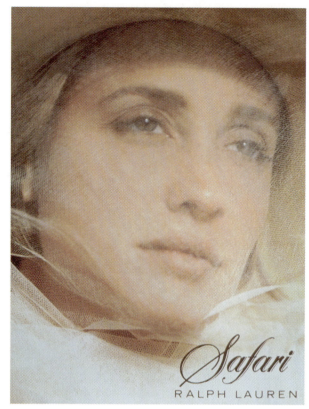
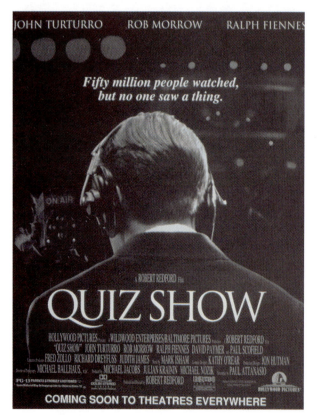

The direction of your models' gaze is of paramount importance.

Top Left: when the model is seen from the front, she addresses your reader directly. This pose is the most efficient way to attract and to hold the attention of your prospective customer.

Top Right: the model shown in three-quarter pose can suggest great delicacy: the modesty of a young girl, a purity and fragility of sentiment. According to Péninou, the skillful photographer is able in this way to avoid brittleness or defiance in the gaze.

Bottom: the model seen from the back appears to be shunning contact. This is a pose normally to be avoided. In our example, the film's original poster showed the main actor from behind. After a slow start at the box-office, it was decided to produce a second poster showing the actor from the front.

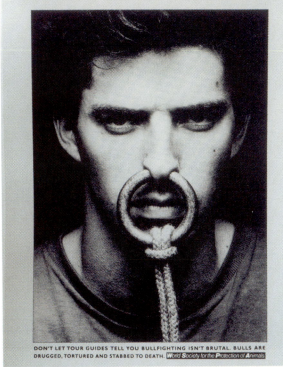

Top:

The nose is first and foremost associated with the sense of smell. Odors can of course have a positive effect on the nose, as is seen in some of McDonald's advertising

Bottom:

One can establish parallels between humans and animals. Cattle-breeding, for example, can be suggested by manipulating the nose of your model.

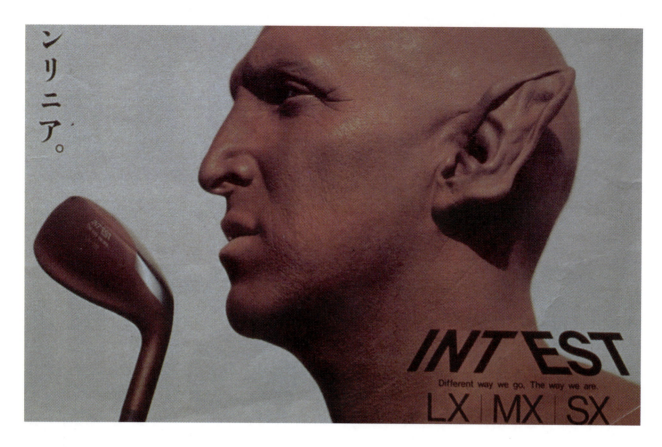

Ears are, of course, intimately associated with hearing. They can evoke both the reception of sound and the refusal to listen.

In popular culture, both Satan and extraterrestrial beings are endowed with pointed red ears, while gifted children have ears that protrude.

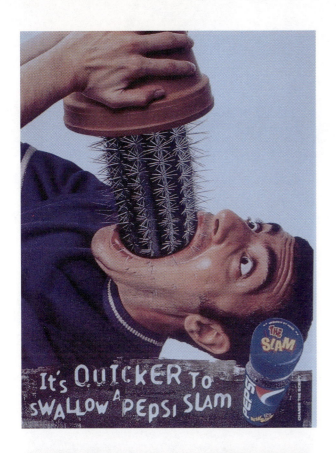

Top:

The mouth is among the most expressive parts of the body. It is through the mouth that one both speaks and eats.

Bottom:

When the mouth is obstructed or otherwise made invisible, it can neither express, nor be heard.

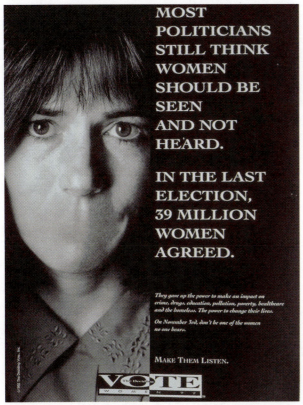

77

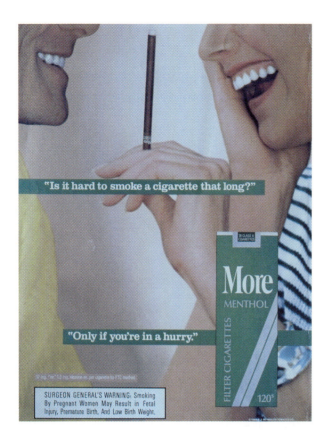

Since the very basis of advertising lies in the constant search for happiness, you can never pay too-close attention to the smile. Go ahead and show plenty of laughter and white teeth. The smile is the expression most often exploited by image-based advertising. It is without equal in expressing pleasure and satisfaction.

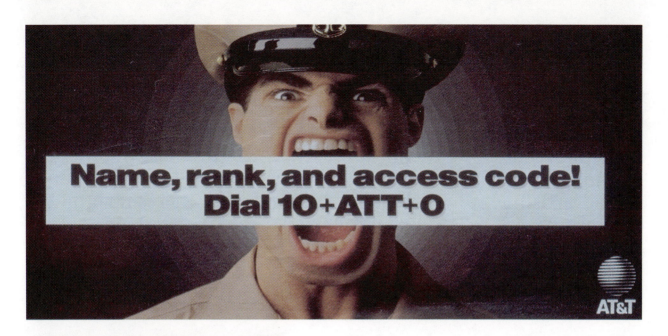

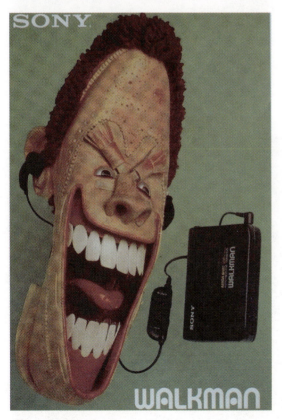

Teeth are an extremely dynamic and powerful symbol. They express psychological health and the joy of living.

If you wish to suggest a ravenous appetite, illustrate your ad with teeth ravenously biting into food.

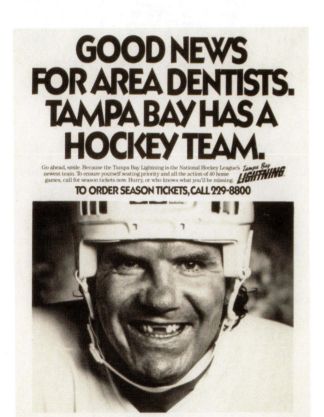

You can surprise your reader by showing teeth that are yellow, pointed, or broken. Occasionally, take a further step towards the peculiar by depicting false teeth.

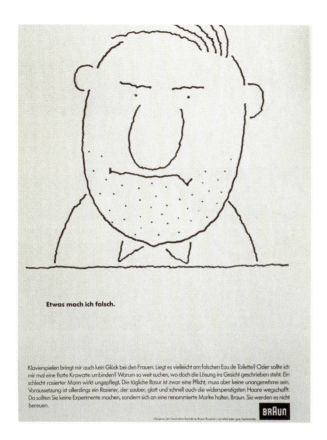

Top:

In rare cases, give an impression of sadness with a drooping lower lip.

Bottom:

A yawn will always suggest boredom. For obvious reasons, it is an image little favored by advertisers.

Top:

The tongue is a very expressive part of the face. It can be displayed or poised to savor an appetizing dish.

Bottom:

Suggest danger: show a snake's tongue.

Bitten lips or fingers that brush against lips transmit important sexual signals.

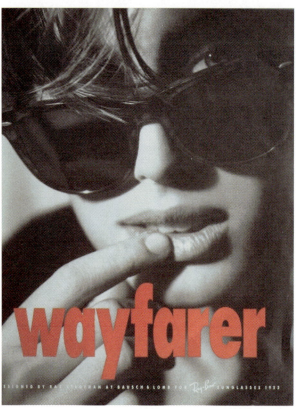

Top:

The neck allows the head to move and to look around. Visually, as with all other parts of the body, it can be shortened or lengthened as if by magic.

Bottom:

The neck is an important erogenous zone. In keeping with the traditional way of seeing the sexes, you will want to endow the man with a solid neck, while giving the woman a neck which is long and slender. Never hesitate to bare the neck in order to direct attention to its beauty and its grace.

Top: when you wish to give a man a more masculine appearance, increase the width of the shoulders or display muscular arms.

Bottom: like the neck, the arms can also be magically lengthened in order to create a strong image.

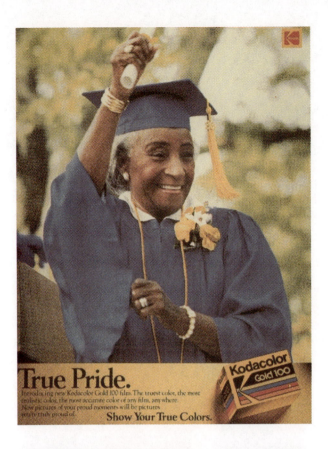

The uplifted arm can either suggest victory or express the idea of surprise.

Crossed arms symbolize an attitude of determination.

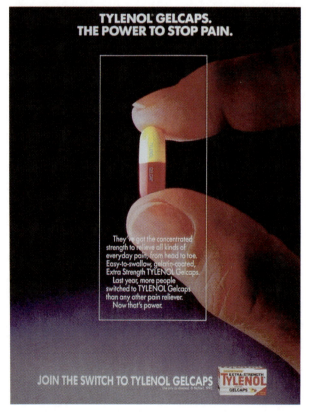

Advertisers love hands and fingers. In addition to providing the advertising photograph with a meaningful suggestion of human presence, they also serve to point out the product.

According to Pierre Martineau, ad images that count on some form of human presence — whether this be a face, an arm, or a leg — succeed in attracting twice as much attention as do ads from which all suggestion of the human body is absent.

By showing hands on a forehead or on the cheeks, you express surprise.

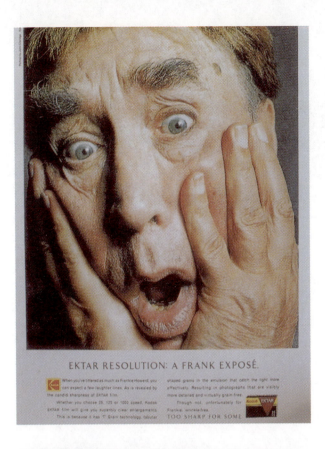

The handshake is particularly well-suited for selling speciality products to the upscale market. Being somewhat ceremonious in character, the handshake expresses agreement and good fellowship.

Joined hands express a servile attitude. In some cases, they can also suggest sexual meanings.

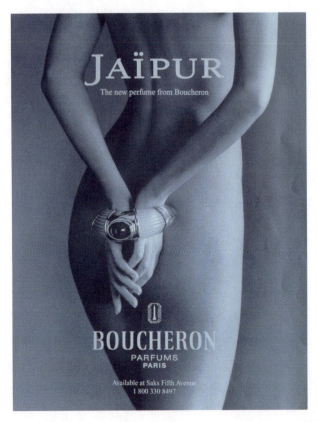

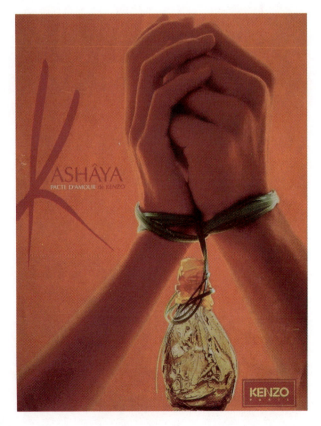

Point the thumb upwards to show that all goes well, or downwards to suggest the contrary.

It is always possible to shock or to insult by raising the middle finger.

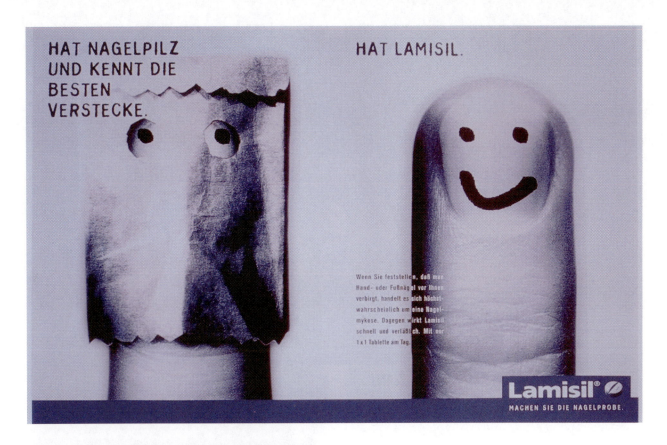

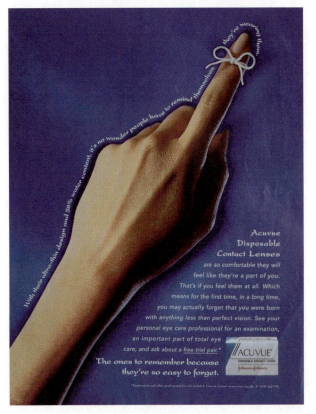

Top:

To inject some originality, cleverly disguise the fingers in your ad as small characters.

Bottom:

Knot a thread around the finger to create a failsafe reminder.

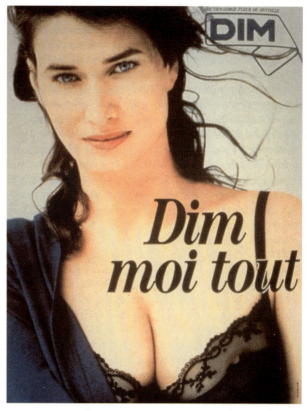

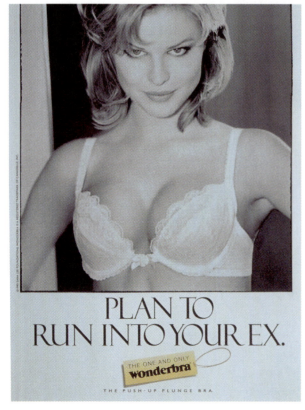

Ads often include the picture of a slender woman with a firm and well-developed bust. This is, of course, no accident.

The female breast, being an important visual stimulus, transmits a sexual signal that appeals significantly to men.

For this reason, it is advisable always to round out the form of the breasts slightly more than is natural. Take care to improve the line by use of a bra or by positions that you may have your models assume.

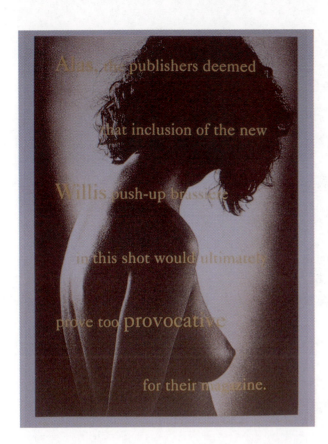

Some ads, particularly in Europe, can show bare-breasted women without shocking anyone. In North America however, it is wiser to leave more to the imagination, thereby showing respect for the sensibilities of your reader.

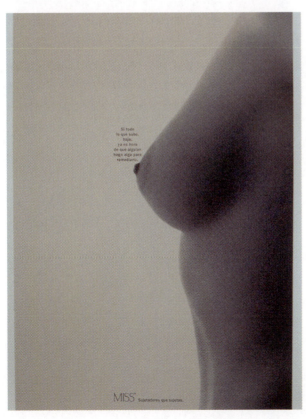

Calvin Klein Underwear

Your thighs may be too thunderous, too saddle-baggy, too thin, too jiggly, too cottage-cheesy (large curd), too hereditary or just too much like the "Before" in a "Before/After" ad. But with Dep styling products, at least you can have your hair the way you want it.

Make the most of what you've got. Dep

You have several ways of attracting the attention of your reader to the bust-line of your models without actually undressing them. You can cover them partially, obstruct their view by means of the placement of objects, hide them with hands, or employ judicious camera angles.

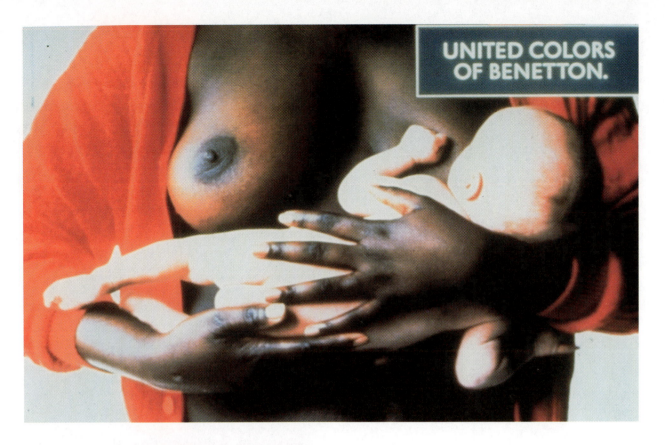

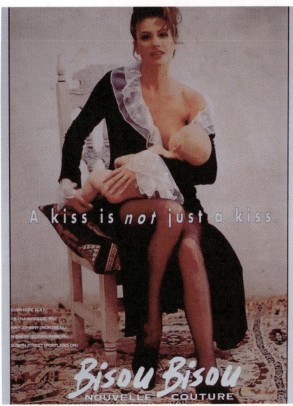

Breast feeding is a powerful image of motherhood, security, and well-being. It is also a gesture replete with cultural meaning.

Several magazines throughout the world therefore refused to give Benetton (see above) advertising space in their pages. In certain cases, it was felt that this type of photography was indecent, while in other cases it was seen as racist. At times, it was even seen as both.

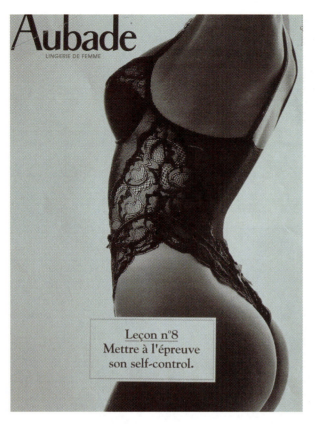

Top:

The bare backs of the woman and the man introduce a discrete form of eroticism. With this view, you get to offer your readers a glance at an expanse of the body's surface sufficiently broad to suggest nakedness, while simultaneously abstaining from the display of precise sexual details. By arching your model's back, you show off the buttocks. The back then takes on a more strongly sexual connotation.

Bottom:

In an ad image, a back which is arched backwards to an unusual degree suggests the business's capacity for adaptation. A variant consists in showing legs joined behind the head. This type of image has been used by numerous firms.

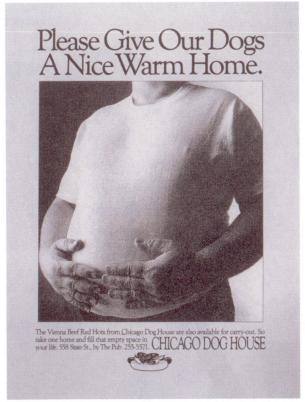

In a society that prizes slimness, the protruding belly is a sign of slackness. Heavy or obese persons are, symbolically speaking, generally seen as miserable, brutish, or corrupt. Their corpulence is seen as a result either of greed or of privilege.

In advertising, there is no object more vivid or more beautiful than the human body when it is both tall and slender. Slimness and youth suggest vivacity, both physical and mental. This is why ads based upon depictions of the body will invariably show men with well developed biceps, abdominal muscles and thighs, and women with a firm bust, smooth hips, and long, slender legs. The presence of strong, prominent abdominal muscles is a sign of good bodily condition. If, for the purposes of advertising, the display of a lax stomach is undesirable, showing the well-muscled one is extremely favorable.

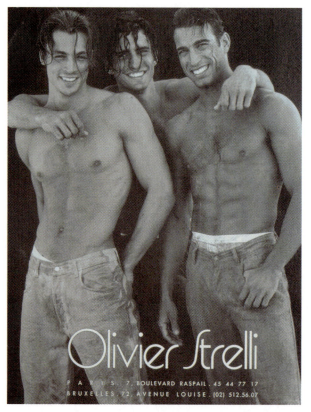

Graphically, suggest slenderness and lightness by using blank spaces or by balancing objects.

It can often be to your advantage to abstain from filling in all the space in your ad. In addition to isolating your titles, your copy, and your images, the use of blank space engenders contrast, thus helping you to set off your products favorably. In addition to this, white is the lightest of all colors, closely followed by light blue. This is why airlines usually use white for the cabins of their aircraft: it gives the impression that the plane itself is light and correspondingly easy to operate.

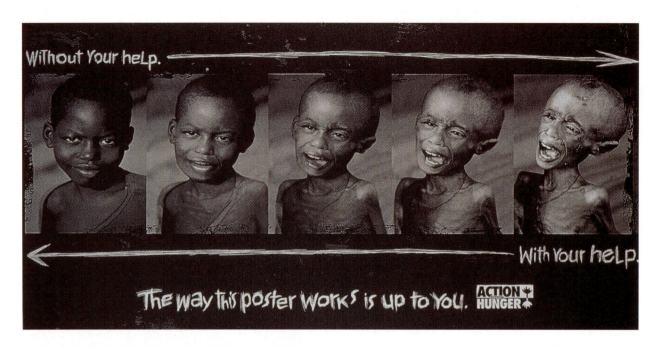

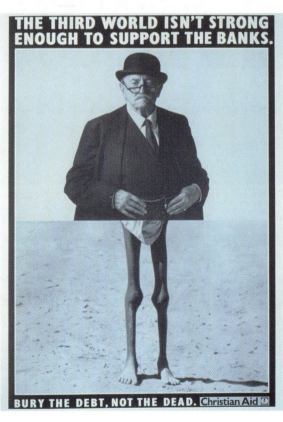

Of course, one must avoid confusing slenderness with malnutrition. The thin African with the bloated stomach is a shock image used by charity campaigns seeking emergency aid for the victims of malnutrition.

Our society's attitudes towards the handicapped are curiously ambivalent. Since the paraplegic does not correspond to the physical norms of his society, he is perceived as marginal. At the same time, handicapped persons are, on the whole, living testimony to the constant need to struggle in order to succeed. For this reason, symbolically, they have a floating, intermediate status.

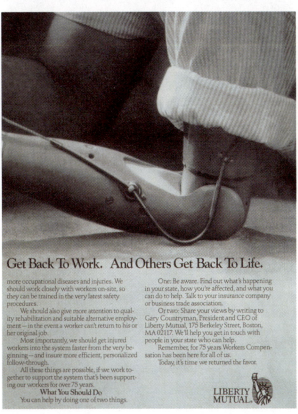

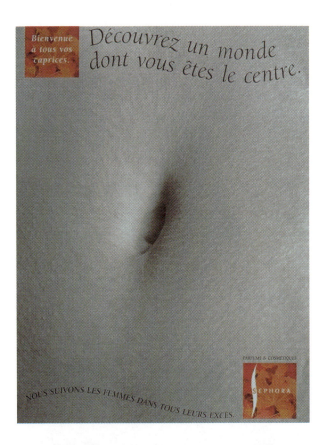

In your images of the female midriff, give preference to the vertically-formed navel. Resembling a bodily orifice, the female navel has always served as an evocation of the female genitalia. Consequently, by presenting a vertical navel, you strengthen the genital symbolism of this bodily detail.

A jewel fastened to the navel suggests lust and the pursuit of sexual pleasure.

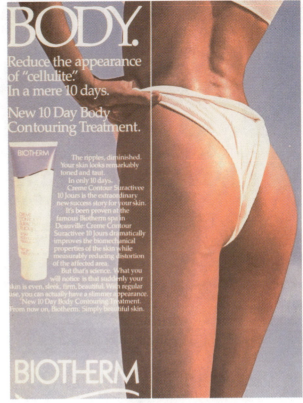

Buttocks are an important erotic emblem. They constitute a markedly erotic zone, quite as much in the case of the male as in that of the female.

Attract attention to female buttocks by showing an arching back, close-fitting pants, and skirts cut to set off the contours of the buttocks. With male models, show firm, solid buttocks, both compact and small, but always muscular.

When it comes to questions of bodily position and movement, anything relating to the hips is feminine. A dance, for example, that accentuates the movement of the hips is clearly sexual in character.

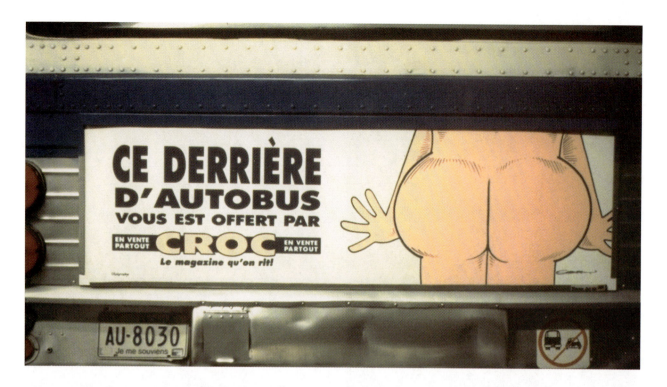

You can gently mock the buttocks of men or women by exposing them directly or by having them pinched or kissed.

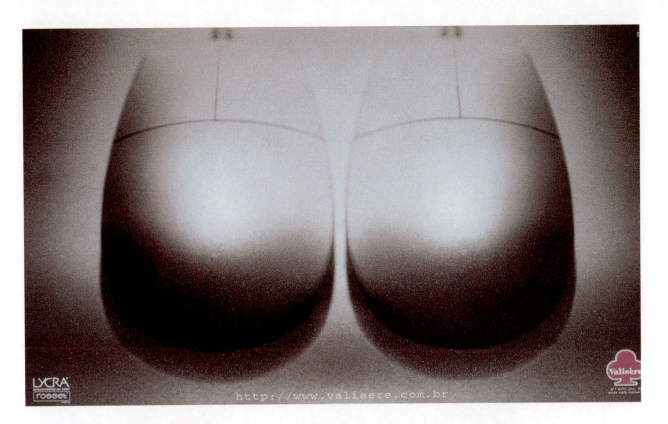

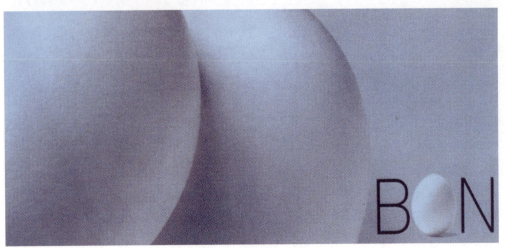

It can be advantageous to exploit the natural resemblance that exists between certain areas of the body, on one hand, and certain fruits or objects, on the other.

Shock images showing persons lowering their pants in order to display their buttocks have, curiously, made their appearance in European advertising. From a North-American point of view however, this kind of imagery is risky business and should be avoided.

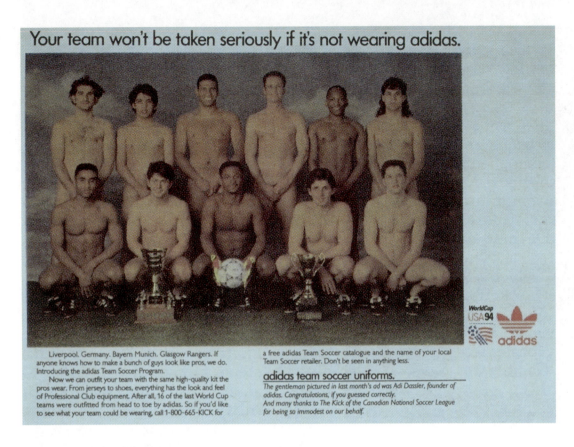

These days, advertisers take it for granted that the genital organs must remain covered, although this covering can be accomplished in all sorts of ways.

Position your models in such a way that the view of the sexual organs will be obstructed. Use angles or compositions that suggest nudity or that reveal only certain parts of the body.

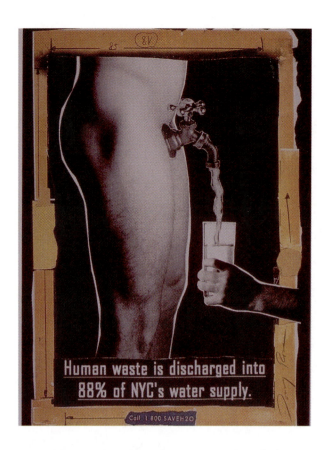

Sometimes, for the sake of originality and in order to spice up your ad, you may suggest that genital organs have been modified. By means of a pencil, for example, transform a woman into a man.

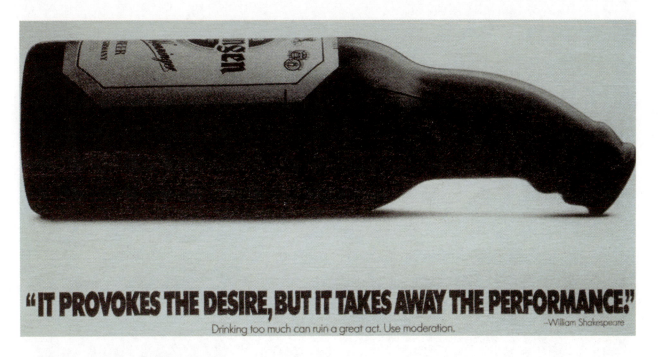

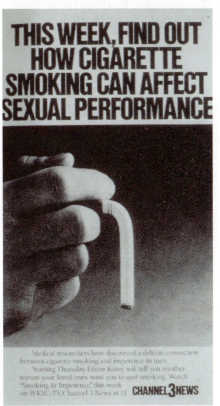

Refer implicitly to the genitals by showing the evocative form of a cactus, a cucumber, a bottle, a cigarette, or a mushroom.

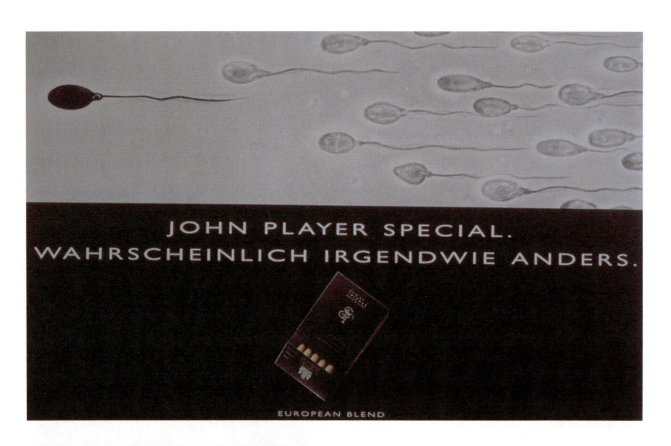

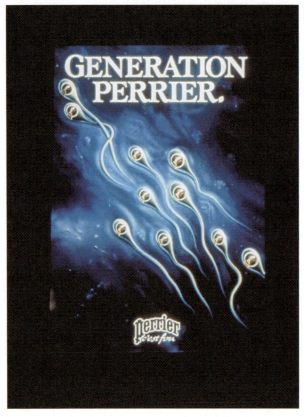

Illustrate your ads with pictures of different aspects of the sexual function, such as that of sperm in pursuit of an ovum.

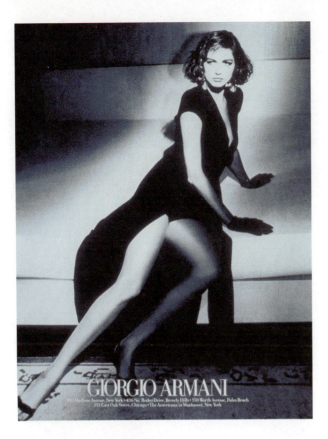

Legs are considered to be symbols of stability and strength. For this reason, it is always a good idea to show girls with unusually long legs and men with extremely muscular ones.

The erotic impact produced by long feminine legs is considerable. By emphasizing this characteristic, you can make your female models sexier and more attractive. This impact can be reinforced by the high heeled shoe, which lengthens the leg by a few centimeters. The short skirt also emphasizes the length of the leg.

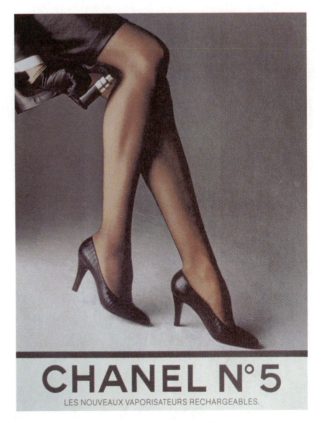

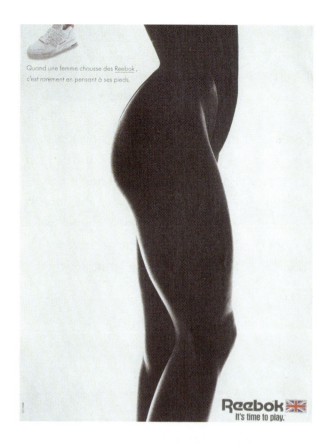

Top Left:

Women's and men's legs are particularly attractive when they are muscular.

Top Right:

Give your models a look of stability and of self-assurance by having them adopt a solid, well-balanced posture, with legs parted in the manner of the cow-boys of the Hollywood screen.

Bottom:

Sagging pants suggest discomfort. Lowered pants suggest deprivation.

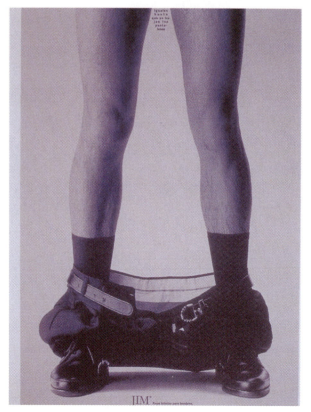

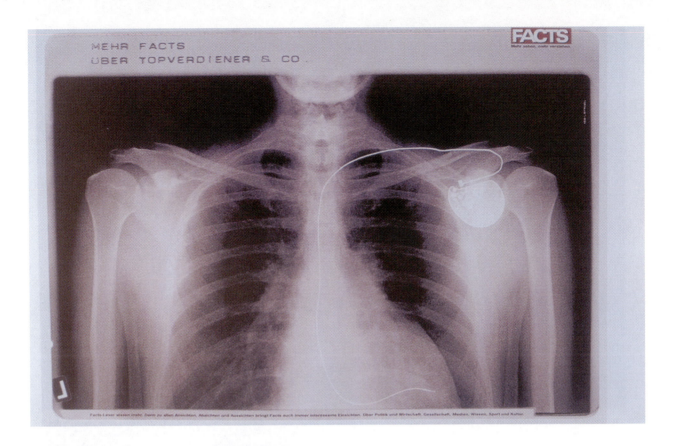

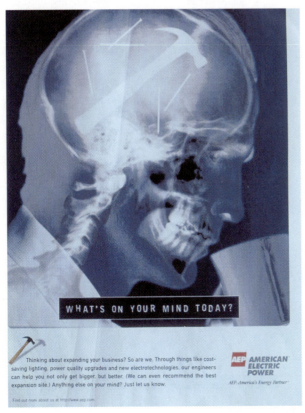

Despite its limited appeal, the human skeleton can sometimes be used. Depending on your message, bone and muscles can either impart a gruesome atmosphere to your images, or they can make them look scientific.

5

BRAND NAMES

To nail down the identity of your product, give it a successful brand name. A product's name is its signature; it conveys an image.

When you are trying to characterise a new product, make its name short, easy to pronounce, and easy to memorize. Choose a name that includes one or more of the letters b, c, d, g, k, p, or t. Linguists call these letters "explosives", because they provoke a burst of air when they are pronounced. A researcher at Michigan State University has discovered that 172 of the 200 best-selling brands in the U.S. use at least one explosive consonant. Among these are Burger King, Cadillac, Coca-Cola, Colgate, Crest, Crisco, Kodak, Kraft, Tide, and Toyota.

Find a name that positions your product in peoples' minds. The name "Budget" for a moderately priced car-rental business, or the name "Arctic Power" for a cold-water detergent, are good examples of names that position products efficiently.

To build up your image, also be attentive to your logo. With enough creativity, you can even place your logo at the center of your product's brand identification. More than a simple accessory, the logo then becomes the central reference point of your advertising campaign and the driving force of your ads.

See also: wealth and culture

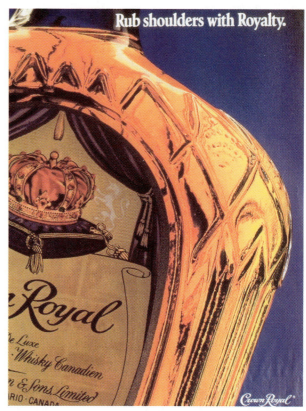

Some graphic designers feel that a product's name and logo should not take up too much space, and so they often tuck the logo away into a small corner of their ads. This is often a mistake.

In reality, the best way to increase familiarity with a brand name is to use close-ups on the product's packaging. In addition to attracting attention to your product, this technique will always help your reader remember it at the time of purchase. Moreover, it has been noticed that the close-up itself injects an element of prestige into the ad.

6

CELEBRITIES

Advertising very frequently uses well-known persons to sell all sorts of products. This, of course, is not an accident. Ads that use celebrity testimonials generally pay handsome dividends. One study that was carried out among 30,000 consumers has shown that, in 1986, celebrities appeared in ten out of the twenty-five television commercials that people admired most.

Famous people are not only respected in the context of the activity where they have made their names: on the contrary, they are also highly esteemed just for being famous. Their great interest to the advertiser lies in their capacity to promote identification with the product. They also incarnate a care-free life-style that seems almost within everyone's grasp.

There are several reasons for using the image of a famous person:
- When the particular celebrity whom you have chosen to use strongly communicates the character of your product
- When your spokesperson is perceived as an expert in the field, as is Wayne Gretzky, for example, for Daoust ice-skates
- When your ad targets young people
- When you are seeking to produce a lively and enjoyable ad
- When you are in the field of institutional communication
- When your target audience is non-specific

In any case, whatever the ad and whatever the product, the objective is to attract the consumer's attention and to associate your product with some key values such as spirit, courage, or adventure.

Interestingly, yesterday's movie-stars are one of advertising's great assets. Not only are they extremely well-known, they are universally loved and admired.

Charged with the responsibility of praising this or that product, Elvis Presley or Marylin Monroe need not explain that they use it. In fact, they need do no more than appear with the product, thus providing the ad with critical visibility.

Their power resides in their mythical capacity to engender identification. They are a transcendent part of everyone's familiar world, and as such they combine rare qualities.

The way many ads persuade is by appealing to memories, by reminding us of a departed screen idol or of the nuance of a feeling. Take the case of James Dean: dead at 24 years of age, this movie star continues to haunt ad images, incarnating the feelings and values of a period and a culture.

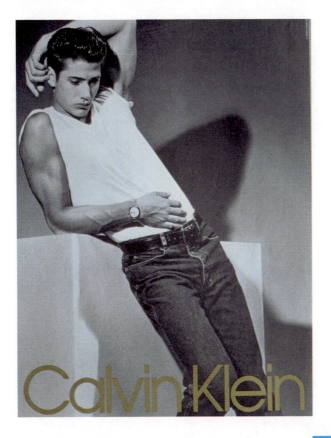

Sometimes an ad campaign can use the "by-products" of fame: a portrait or a silhouette.

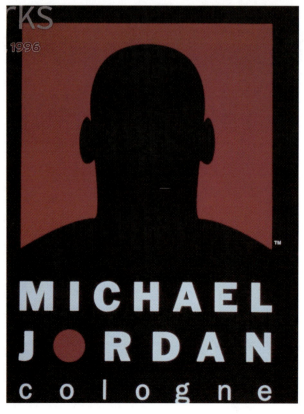

The world of professional sports is a very important part of show-business. It has its own star-system. Here we see the professional hockey player Patrick Roy and the basketball superstar Michael Jordan.

Contrary to what is often believed, advertisers resort quite frequently to politicians and soldiers to illustrate their ads.

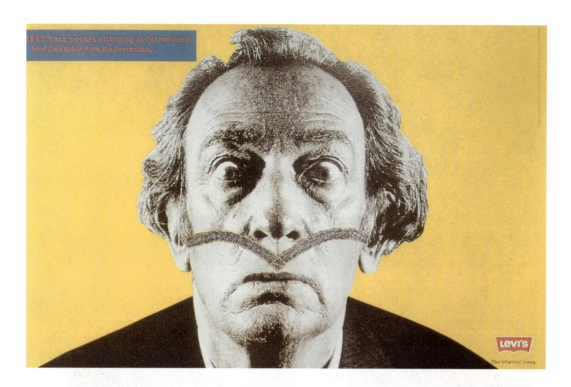

Actors and professional athletes are not the only stars. You can also use writers, explorers, painters, singers, or scientists. Here we see Salvador Dali and Albert Einstein.

7

CHILDREN

As often as possible, it is a good idea to include images of children in your ads. Just like babies, children are an important and highly profitable theme for the successful promotion of all sorts of products.

Each time that you show your product in the hands of a child, your ad will receive greater attention and be more thoroughly memorized than it would have been if you had chosen to present it in some other way.

In order for your images of children to be successful, they should always seize the positive connotations associated with the idea of growth. Make your photographs include objects that are generally and traditionally associated with childhood, and compose your image around activities such as the series of "firsts" that mark the stages of development in a child's life.

In addition, it is of paramount importance that you have fathers participate in children's games and education. Twenty years ago, fathers hardly appeared at all in advertising. But since then, things have changed considerably. Nowadays, society admires fathers who are intensely involved in the lives of their children. This means that, in your visual, Dad will be teaching the kids how to fish, for example, or how to fly a kite. He will also be totally capable of expressing his feelings and of having fun.

See also: the family

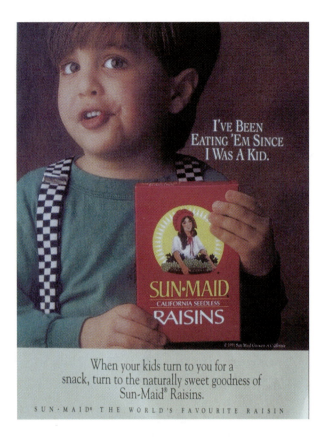

Advertisers often call upon children to sell their products. Children have the advantage of winning the everyone's attention: women and men, the old and the young. Besides, the presence of children in the ad is particularly effective when it comes to selling products specifically aimed at that age group.

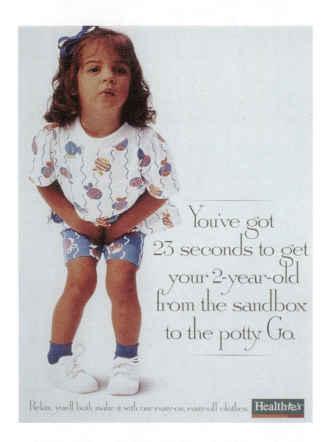

Never underestimate the punch that children can bring to your advertising. The sight of children, no matter what they happen to be doing, invariably evokes sympathetic feelings. Be sure to make use of the full range of symbols associated with the process of growing up.

Childhood is the world of games and of play. Games bring children together, develop their skills, and teach competition. Throughout these years, children feel the need to play in order to understand the world and adapt themselves to it. Adults, too, are sensitive to the importance of games.

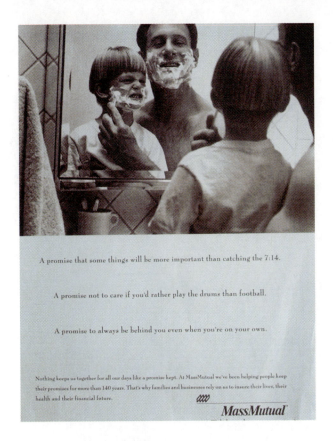
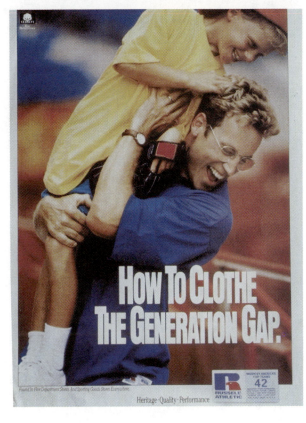

Advertising has long avoided showing "emotional" scenes of fathers with children. But fashions have begun to change. The first big ad campaign to use fathers and children together was the one that Kodak developed in the eighties. The images associated with this campaign generated very high rates of attention. And they later inspired the new trend towards the portrayal of attentive, caring fathers.

For obvious reasons, a basic link exists between children and school. If you want to represent the classroom, show it in a familiar light and with simplified imagery.

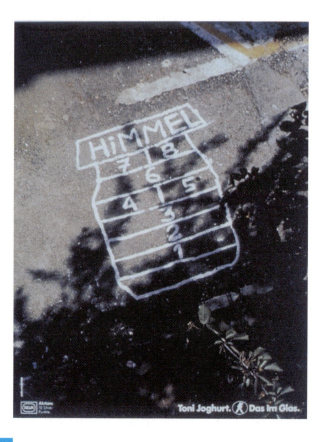

8

THE CITY

Nowadays, the city is the backdrop against which the characters in your ad will normally be projected. Modern society is witness to an increasingly rapid urban development, and your images cannot stand outside this very important trend.

Today, everything happens in the city. The city is a way of life. Also, young people, born for the most part in cities, have very strong ties to urban culture. Of course, the rural world continues to exist, but always as a symbol of the past.

As far as spatial organization is concerned, the differences between the city and the countryside are immense. In cities, houses and apartment-buildings abound; crowds are everywhere; office-towers are the ubiquitous symbols of the central business district.

Cities appear as the places where resources are densely gathered. Every city is a cross-roads. Questions of transportation are central, and the different ethnic groups are numerous.

Today, the symbol par excellence of the city is no longer London or Paris. Centers of business and of intellectual life have gone elsewhere. Henceforth, it is to the U.S., and especially to New York, that you will look to find the typical forms of the modern city.

See also: the countryside and America

In advertising, disagreements over the various possible meanings of the city are a thing of the past. Today, the city is a way of life.

The city is fast becoming a total experience, especially for the younger generations. Of course, the countryside continues to exist, but, more and more, only as a reminder of an earlier time.

Dramatize the spectacle of traffic. Emphasize the fantastic side of this typically urban phenomenon by showing busy intersections and broad boulevards.

9

THE COUNTRYSIDE

The rural environment forms a homogeneous whole, a world unto itself, quite in harmony with the needs and the purposes of the advertiser. In reassuring contrast to the harried tension of urban life, and in contrast especially to the growing reality of social conflict, the countryside is an oasis of peace and harmony.

To evoke security and rural stability, use an image either of the forest or of the individual tree, laying particular emphasis on the depiction of its branches and its leaves. You can also symbolize all of nature as a combination of earth and water by showing rivers, ponds, or waterfalls.

Work a rural vision into your ad by showing a village, a small house, a general store, or a church. Better yet, depict a farm with its wooden fences and people at work.

At times, it is useful to contrast the city and the countryside. If you want to stress green spaces, show the city in an unfavorable light. Reveal it to be a cold and repellent place, and ascribe liberating qualities to the out-of-doors.

At a symbolic level, suggest comfort and peacefulness by combining tones of green and blue. By using a green logo, you can freshen up and modernize the overall look of your business.

See also: the city

In picturing the countryside, it is important that you encourage the desire for nature and freedom. The village, the country house, and the barn are intended to beguile and lure your reader with suggestions of harmony and repose.

Be sure to show farm life in all its guises. The farmer typically has a strong attachment to his traditions. His life revolves around the soil, the weather, and the changing seasons.

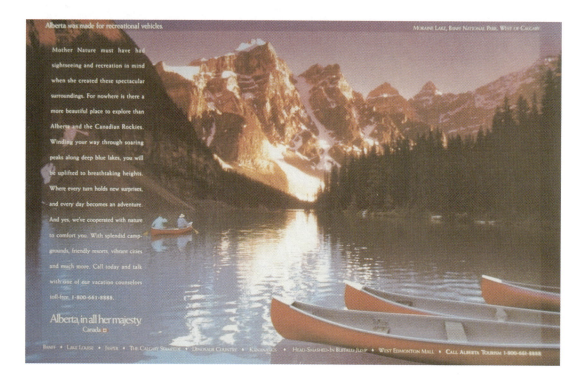

Top: get at the heart of the countryside by depicting all sorts of bodies of water. The rural universe is characterized by rest, by the sound of a waterfall, and by the reassuring calm of a lake or a river.

Bottom: as a vertical barrier, the mountain circumscribes men's aspirations. Climbing it, however, signifies conquest.

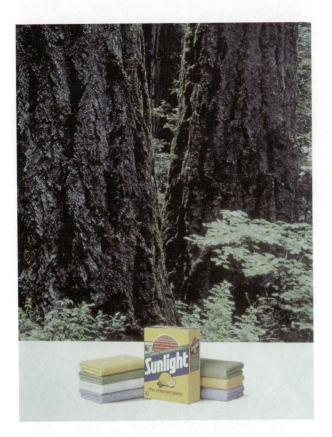

Suggest security and the peaceful stability of country life by combining tones of green and blue. If you want to evoke the beauty and vivacity of nature, use images of the forest and of trees with their branches and leaves. The tree carries the symbolic weight of grandeur and majesty. It is synonymous with strength. The tree also offers comfort and support.

Furthermore, green is an invitation to tranquillity. In fact, it can lower blood-pressure. It is a symbol of freshness and natural health.

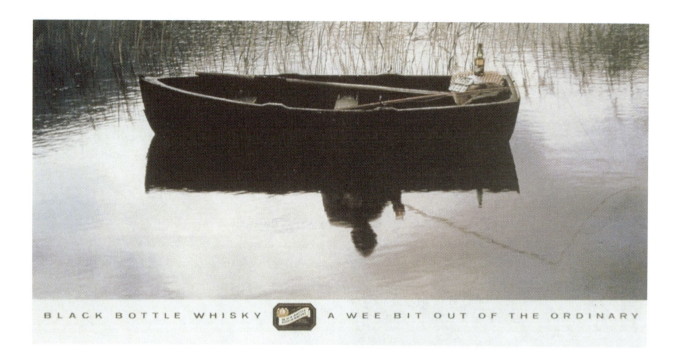

Since it is increasingly threatened by industrial civilization and the encroaching urban environment, nature is often seen as a clean and healthy retreat and a most desirable place to live. The sporting activities that one can enjoy there are healthy and vivifying.

10

CULTURE

To enrich your ads, refer to images associated with culture. In advertising, a good product must immediately bear witness to the consumer's cultivated taste and refinement. The ideal consumer will be seen as wealthy and conservatively educated at the best schools.

Place books, encyclopaedias and newspapers around your product. You can also display your product in a museum or in an art exhibition. In some cases, refer directly to paintings by Rembrandt or Van Gogh; modify an original artwork by inserting the image of your product into it.

In your images, show objects, scenes and people closely related to the world of music. Do not hesitate to use musical instruments, whether these be strings, wind instruments, or instruments of percussion.

The cultivated man, by definition, knows how to appreciate what is good and desirable. He drinks champagne and fine spirits. Refinement also suggests that one consume such delicacies as caviar and that one smoke a pipe or cigar.

Among the privileges that cultivated people enjoy, freedom from being harassed by time is certainly one of the most precious. These people therefore have an increasingly sought-after advantage over the ordinary employee: that of the enjoyment of leisure, symbolized by a game of chess, for example.

When you want to refer to culture and to the intellectual life-style, associate your product with old books and other specialized reading-material.

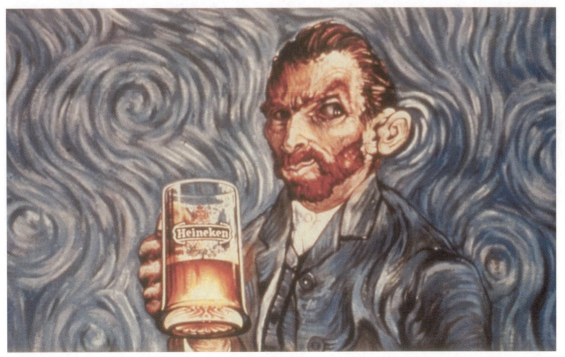

The art is an important manifestation of culture. By showing an old master painting, or indeed by borrowing its style, you hearken back emotionally to high culture, thus demonstrating the value of your product through association.

No work is more reinterpreted and transformed by graphic artists than is the famous Mona Lisa.

To suggest good taste, use musical instruments, whether these be strings, wind instruments, or percussion. Show objects, scenes and people closely related to the world of music.

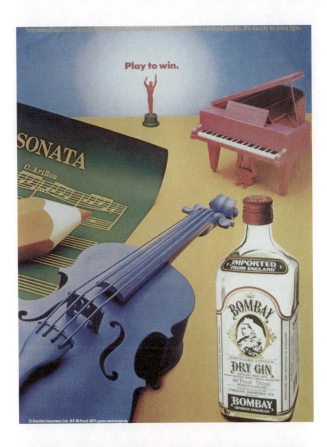

Dance slippers and other accoutrements of the ballet are sure signs of sensitivity and a cultivated sense of refinement.

11

DEATH

Even if images of death obtain high rates of attention from consumers, I personally suggest that it is best to avoid them.

Death, as the completion of life, is a source of anguish and is always seen as frightening. Symbolically, it is a closing. Given this, death cannot be considered to have much to offer the advertiser.

If on the other hand you should decide to show death and associate it with your product, you will certainly find yourself in violation of the unwritten code of advertising that requires, at all times, a happy ending, a beautiful smile, and a carefree life-style. With death in the picture, you cannot avoid attracting hostile attention. Tread carefully.

And yet: advertising is, after all, created in society's image, and this image, we must admit, is often a violent one. The death that one illustrates may have occurred as the result of accident, murder, or suicide. Blood, bone and detached limbs are gruesome and repulsive in the extreme. Arms, as tools of attack or defense, symbolize potential danger.

The visual conception of any ad portraying death will represent in some way the human condition and will likely constitute a caricature of social life, rendering it monstrous. Such images will be unusual and surprising, sometimes ironic, but in all cases, extremely risky.

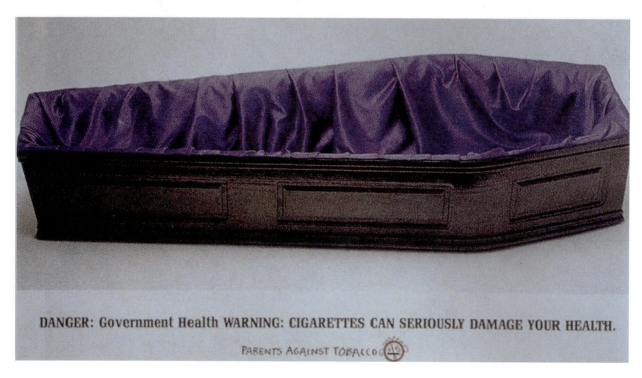

Some ads break current advertising codes by exploring death and mourning. Do they work? Probably not.

For some years now, advertising images have testified to some of life's drama.

Advertising is created in society's image, and this image, we must admit, is often a violent one.

12

THE EARTH

Under the impetus of what is now referred to as the globalization of markets, I would encourage you to consider as never before the use of pictures of the planet Earth.

Make the Earth the centerpiece of your advertising image. Illustrate your ad with a globe, or gather together the flags of several countries.

When you want to surprise your reader, show a planet that is not round. Reshape it, or square it. Better still, bring the continents together so as to evoke the globalization of markets and what McLuhan called in the sixties "the global village".

Among Earth symbols, the sky is unmatched for conveying the idea of power. The sky represents all that is elevated. Since time immemorial, it has been a powerful symbol of ascension and progress.

The water that one associates with the earth evokes freshness, purity, and cleanliness. Water both awakens and rejuvenates. Source of life, agent of renewal, water cleanses and purifies the body.

Fire, as an image, symbolizes passion, most notably the passions of love and anger. Fire is synonymous with life, light, force, and energy.

See also: the future and outer space

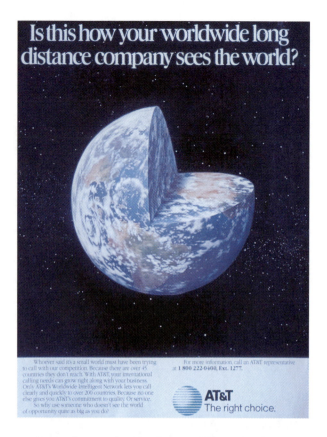

Since Time magazine made the Earth its "man of the year", the picture of the blue planet has been showing up everywhere, including advertising.

The Earth has a double meaning in the advertising image. When you want to express globalization, show the continents united. To surprise and intrigue your reader, you can carve the earth up or modify its shape.

Suggest power by depicting a rough sea. The sea and the ocean have the power to inspire courage. What is more, one can associate water, ice, waves, and the color blue with ideas of freshness, nature, and purity. Water awakens and freshens.

Top:

The blue sky with its white clouds is saturated with positive associations.

Bottom:

The grey or red sky is generally negative.

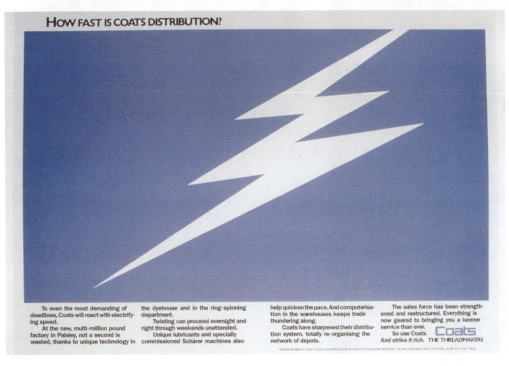

Top: wind and storm reflect instability. An elemental force both fierce and blind, the wind is also an instrument of power. When the wind is up and rain is falling hard, one can be sure that something momentous is about to occur. *Bottom:* powerful and swift, lightning is symbolic of the spark of life. Like the tornado, it transmits energy, and it inspires fear.

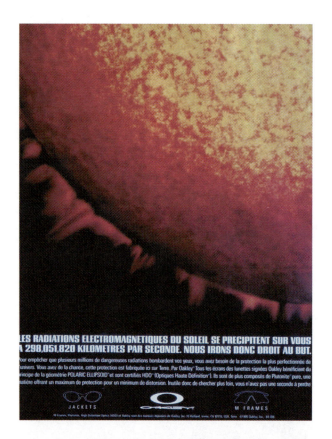

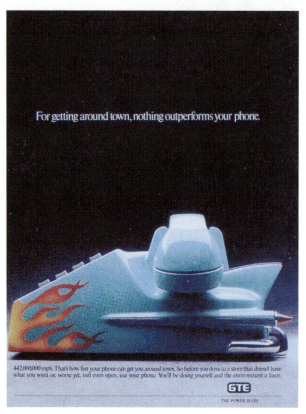

Top:

The sun, as source of light, suggests heat.

Bottom:

The fire on the front of the telephone suggests the energy and robustness of the company. Fire symbolizes both force and energy.

13

THE ELDERLY

In advertising, the elderly often play a secondary role. According to an American study, only three percent of people who appear in advertising can be considered elderly.

Obviously, this near-absence of old people in advertising stands in stark contrast with the size of the ageing population and should be explained. The most likely explanation is the need to conceal whatever disturbs us in a society that idolizes the vigor of youth.

However, we must recognize that the advertising industry has launched an important trend. Older people enjoy financial resources that give them a sizeable appeal to advertisers, particularly in product categories such as those of travel, life insurance, and food and drink.

In the U.S., the senior market potential is now estimated at $800 billion. Taking into account this new reality, I strongly suggest that, for purposes of identification, you use the elderly in your images.

Show the affection that exists between grandparents and their grandchildren, between fathers and their adult sons. Better still, have your models act out the blissful scenes of family life and show a loving elderly couple.

See also: the past and the body

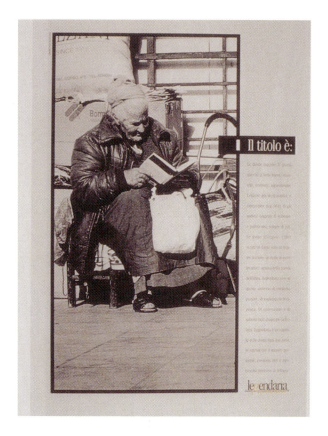
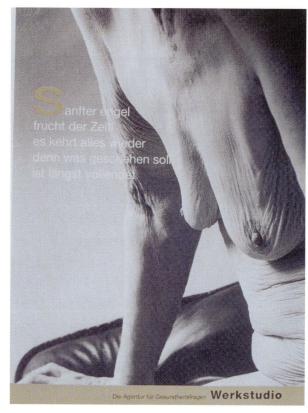
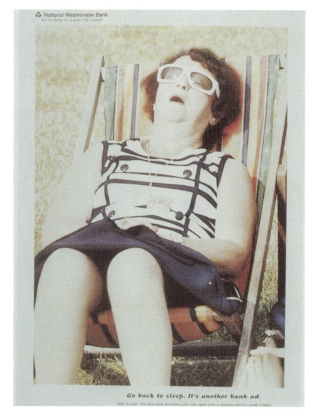

The image of the elderly can arouse fear, since it often suggests solitude, insufficient resources, physical decline, and ridicule.

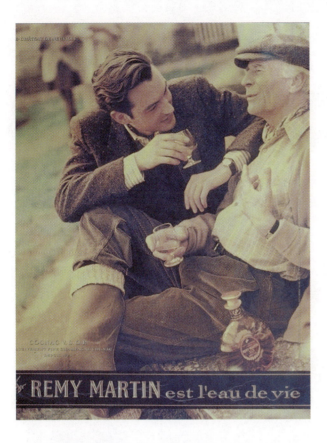

It is important that you manage to express the love and affection that binds grandparents and their grand-children, the father to his adult son, an ageing man to his wife.

By showing the affection that older people have for each other, you literally inject emotional capital into your illustrations. At the same time, you encourage the identification of older persons with the characters shown using your product.

Of course, the falling birth rate and increased life expectancy are having important repercussions on advertising. Nowadays, elderly people are more important than ever to your business. It has therefore become necessary to entice this sector of the population.

Baby-boomers have a remarkable impact on the sale of certain products. Thus, demand for bright colors in lip-stick has begun to decline in North America, while demand for skin-care products is on the rise.

To surprise your reader, show elderly people in situations that point to meanings other than that of age. Show a zest for living, dynamism, and participation in all facets of social life.

14

EXOTICISM

Exoticism is one of advertising's favorite themes. It is closely linked to the quest for the ideal. Exoticism is always associated with the desire to discover and explore those far-off foreign places that promise to take us out of our hum-drum existence.

Pictures of the beach — featuring islands, sand, sea, and sun — are among those that evoke exoticism and freedom from care.

The beach is nevertheless in competition with other places that are able to lay a certain claim to exoticism, places such as Europe, Latin America, Asia, and Africa. Each of these regions of the world conveys a symbolic ambience linked as much to cultural stereotypes as it is to factual reality.

The exoticism that one finds in advertising is generally served up in the form of a setting destined to function as a backdrop. In the words of John Paul Gourevitch, this stereotypical brand of exoticism is of the "post-card" variety. It is not likely to surprise, nor indeed is it intended to do so.

In fact, when all is said and done, your exotic images, in order to be effective, will ultimately have to be clichés. What is important for your purposes is not to imagine a totally new way of looking at the world, but to recreate a place that can be recognized as easily and as readily as possible by your prospective buyer.

Above all else, exoticism is an invitation to adventure. This LA Gear ad reflects the company's desired image, what it would like to symbolize in the consumer's mind — travel and escape.

The search for an unknown desert island is one of the fundamental themes of the advertising image. The island is associated with a carefree existence, with joie de vivre.

Sand, sea, swaying palm trees, the sun and the blue sky express exoticism and a care-free lifestyle. These symbols naturally seem to assure the escape and leisure that your product promises to provide.

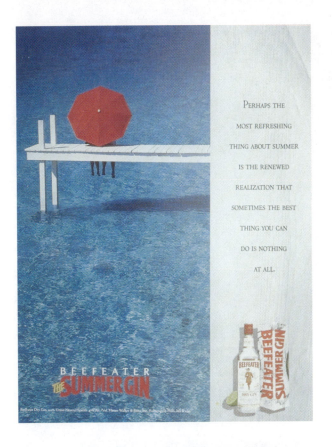

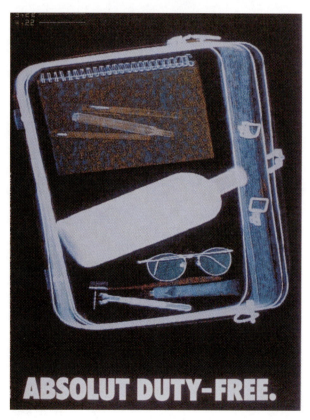

There are certain objects that, in themselves, constitute an invitation to holiday travel: suitcase, beach towel, tanning lotion, etc.

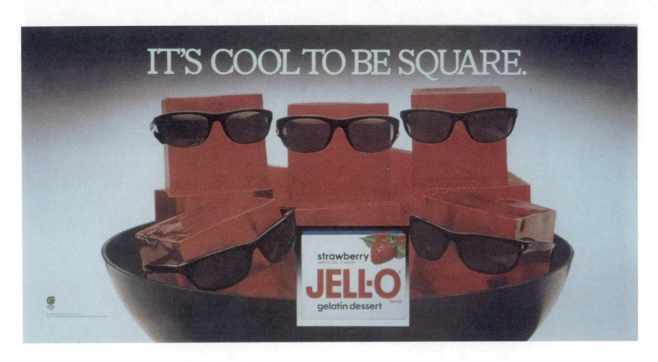

Like other symbols of summertime, sunglasses can serve as a starting-point for building powerful images. In fact, this symbol is particularly pliable: depending on your needs, sunglasses can suggest a tourist visiting sunny climes, a hoodlum, or a movie-star.

From the point of view of symbolic meanings, certain European countries convey a high degree of exoticism, which advertising can put to profitable use.

In addition to such classic symbols as flags, politicians, and famous geographical features, each country possesses its own given image, or trademark, along with a few essential symbols.

A long-established tradition, wisely safeguarded and promoted by the French, has made France the country of luxury, elegance, and supreme good taste.

To judge by current and recent advertising imagery, modern Germany has not yet been entirely successful in ridding itself of associations with its bellicose past. Over fifty years after the end of the Second World War, the swastika and Adolph Hitler are still frequently seen.

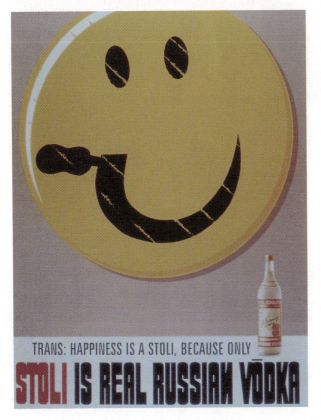

Contrary to the example of other European countries, the ex-USSR has nothing very exotic about it. And yet, since the end of the USSR and since the Communist system was relegated a few years ago to the dustbin of history by its own political leaders, Russia seems to have found it possible to profit somewhat from current events.

The official portrait of the ex-Soviet Union is remarkably stable and unchanging. Four important personages have indelibly marked the country's history: Marx, Stalin, Lenin, and now Gorbatchev. The Soviet flag, with its hammer and sickle, and the figure of the Cossack are also familiar, but should now be seen in irony and used in a more indirect and winking manner.

The exoticism of Latin America can be reduced to one key image: the Mexican dozing beneath his sombrero.

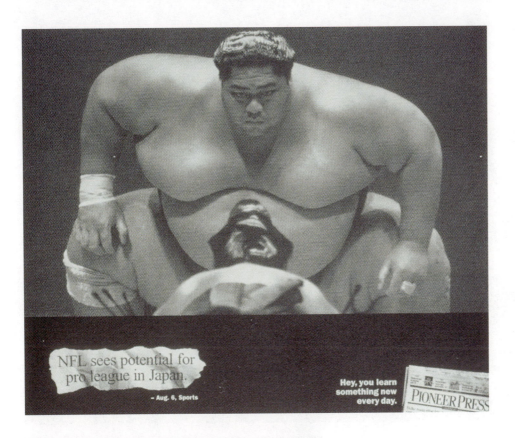

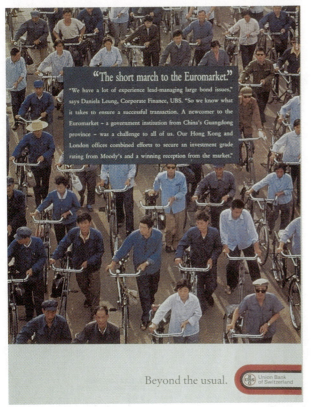

Asia's symbols remain mysterious and therefore somewhat difficult to grasp. The continent's two most prominent countries, Japan and China, have long fascinated westerners.

The formula is very simple. Japan is evoked by its flag, by the faces of its residents, by its geishas, its wrestlers, its samurais, its sushi, its streets filled with neon signs, and by the eternal Mount Fuji.

China is represented by the characters of its written language, the Great Wall, and by the many cyclists that invade the streets of its major cities.

Australia is immediately recognizable with its characteristic geography, boomerang, koala bear, and kangaroo.

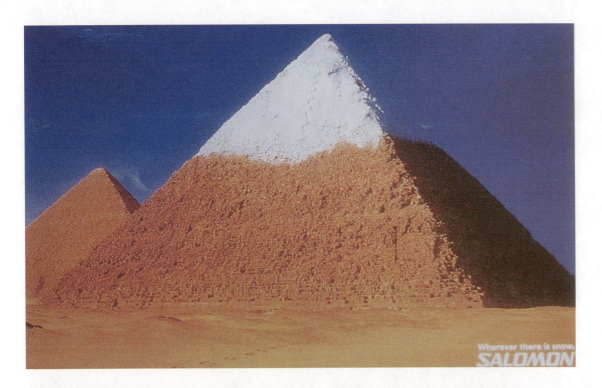

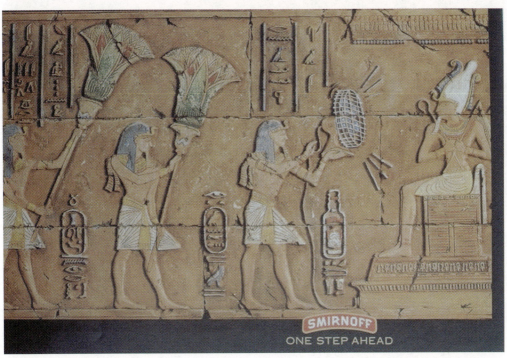

Egypt is the only Arab country to occupy an important place in the imagination of advertising. Indeed, its eternal images are hard to avoid: the pyramids and hieroglyphics.

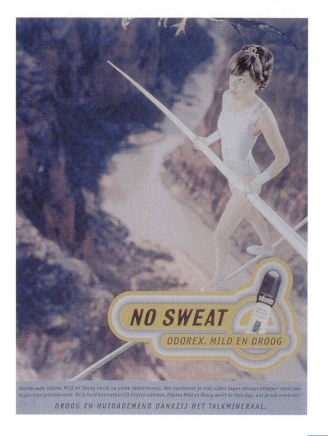

At a more symbolic level, advertisers will sometimes turn to the circus and to the circus environment for the special brand of exoticism that this form of spectacle holds for many people. One need only think of such notable features as the display of death-defying agility and of ever-present danger.

15

THE FAMILY

Despite the steadily climbing divorce rate, one must not imagine that advertising images depicting families are a thing of the past. On the contrary, despite trends elsewhere in society, the family remains advertising's main reference group.

In the face of growing doubts concerning the nature of relationships between men and women, advertising has chosen to juxtapose two family models, one traditional and the other contemporary.

The traditional family lives most often in a one-family house and includes a husband, a wife, and two children, inevitably a boy and a girl separated in age by a few years. A long-haired dog will often appear in the picture.

And yet, the family of the advertising image differs markedly from what it was a mere fifty years ago. The general breakdown of the family institution has given rise to a new model for living. Even the traditional responsibilities that once divided men and women have changed. For example, the father is no longer the sole or even the dominant authority figure. Men are also assuming a greater share of responsibility in the home. What was once paternal authority has largely become a shared parental authority.

See also: babies, children, woman, and man

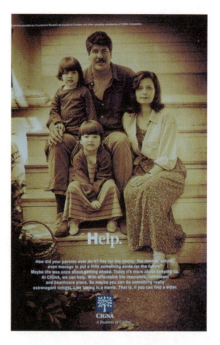

The family remains advertising's main reference group. The traditional family lives most often in a one-family dwelling and includes a husband, a wife, and two children, inevitably a boy and a girl separated in age by a few years. Of course, this idea of the family is sometimes flouted, as is the case with Diesel Jeans ads.

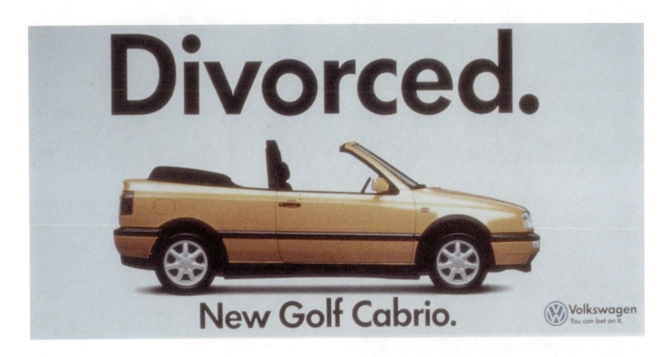

The general breakdown of the family institution has given rise to a new model for living. The climbing divorce rate is certainly responsible for much of the revaluation of the traditional family model. Television advertising is still better suited for capturing this reality than is the print ad.

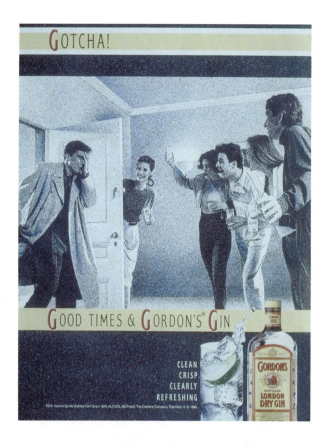

The picture of the "new" family shows how advertising is keeping up with changing times in an attempt to reflect the real-life conditions of the consumer. The new family tends characteristically to interact closely with friends, neighbors and co-workers.

16

FESTIVITIES

Advertising is at the heart of all our annually recurring activities. The rituals that we see in ads reinforce the spirit of holiday celebration, and they go far towards giving us a break from the daily grind. For this reason, the advertiser is well-advised to make full use of the symbols of holiday celebration.

Holidays embody the happiness and good times that are shared among friends and family. For reasons not difficult to understand, the Christmas season is advertising's busy period. Indeed, many businesses realize over fifty percent of their annual turnover at Christmas time.

Christmas is of course personified by the ubiquitous Santa Claus, along with three of his very tangible and well-defined symbols: red suit, white beard, and portly belly. But then, even if he is everybody's favorite character, there is no reason to limit the ad image to illustrations of Santa Claus. Symbols of Christmas can also be found in the Christmas tree, in the ribbons and the gift-wrapping, and in candy canes, to name a few.

In advertising, only the birthday party can match Christmas celebrations in importance. Balloons and party hats, cake and candles, all these will help you to evoke this important ritual of life.

See also: love

Advertising is at the heart of all annually-recurring celebrations: Christmas, Easter, Saint Valentine's Day, etc.

Christmas symbols are numerous and unmistakable: candy canes, wreaths, Christmas stockings, gifts wrapped in paper and ribbon, the tree complete with its lights and ornaments, and of course Santa Clause.

With the introduction of these themes into your images, you will break with everyday reality and instill a festive mood.

17

FICTITIOUS CHARACTERS

Generally speaking, ad campaigns that use a character or an animal as spokesperson for a product get above-average results.

"By developping a character and making him famous," says the advertiser Claude Hopkins, "you make your product famous. People are not interested in corporations. They are interested in people."

Examples of characters that have made their product famous abound. Consider, for example, the following:

- the Raid insect
- Colonel Sanders
- the Yellow Pages finger
- Tony the Tiger
- Mr. Clean
- the Man from Glad
- Aunt Jemima
- Betty Crocker
- the Maytag repairman
- the Esso Tiger
- Chef Boyardee
- the Jolly Green Giant
- the Pillsbury dough boy
- Snap, Crackle, and Pop.

These characters are very effective: in polls conducted in 1985, 93% of American women shoppers could name the familiar bald-headed Mr. Clean, the man who cleans kitchen floors "to the shine", while only 56% could identify then Vice President George Bush.

Today, one of the most famous of all fictitious characters is the clown Ronald McDonald. The creation is the result of a long evolution. The McDonald company's first clown carried, on his head, a tray containing a hamburger, a bag of french-fries, and a milk-shake. His shoes were shaped like small bread-loaves, and his nose resembled a McDonald's paper cup.

McDonald's ad agency originally suggested calling the clown "Archie", before opting for the name "Ronald".

Ronald McDonald made his debut in Washington D.C. in 1963. He was an immediate success. Already by the mid-sixties, McDonald's was staking most of its $500 000 advertising budget on Ronald McDonald. With the opening of each new restaurant, Ronald was called in.

For a while, the company entertained the idea of transforming Ronald into a cow-boy, and then into an astronaut, in order to symbolize progress and changing times. Ultimately, however, the clown image was kept, so that the character might continue appealing to children.

And yet, McDonald's adapts to specific markets. For example, in Japan, McDonald's is called "Makudonaldo".

18

THE FUTURE AND OUTER SPACE

If you want to convince consumers to purchase products that are capable of taking them into the third millennium, take advantage of the symbols of science and of science fiction. By using futuristic themes, you can promote and set off your product, while at the same time giving it an aura of adventure.

Widespread illustrations of the future bear witness to a fascination with everything new. This interest is based on the somewhat confused and yet widely held idea according to which there exists such a thing as universal progress, such that anything new and modern is clearly superior to anything old.

Thus, for many people, futur time is a bearer of ultimate hope. Advertising therefore offers a peek into the solutions to current problems. These solutions are the familiar ones of steadily developping knowledge, technical innovation, and scientific research.

Insist on the necessity of confronting the future and of taking up the challenges of the year 2000. The conquest of space has proven that the infinite can be made accessible to discovery. Your images will prove to be all the more spectacular since frontiers between science and science fiction are becoming increasingly blurred.

See also: the past and the earth

NOTHING ESCAPES AGFA FILM

Represent outer space through the illustration of technical equipment, either real or fictional, such as rockets, lunar modules, all-terrain vehicles, satellites, orbit stations, space shuttles, the Star Trek ship "Enterprise", and flying saucers.

On the cosmic scale, use depictions of the universe, of galaxies, and of the solar system. They express what is infinitely large and recall to the human mind the relatively small place we occupy in the universe.

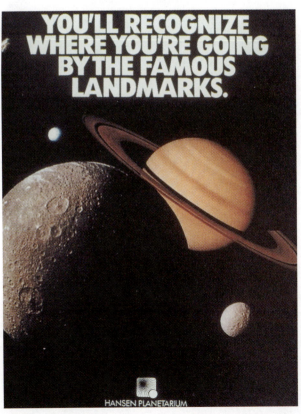

Be sure to make full use of the visual effects of pictures of the planet Saturn and its rings. Indeed, pictures of Saturn are without equal in evoking the character of the celestial bodies that are just waiting to be conquered.

The sense of progress symbolized by images of future cities is rooted in a blind faith in the future. The future seems to be filled with promise, and it provides an especially evocative means for escaping from everyday reality.

Insist on the necessity of confronting the future and of taking up the challenges of the year 2000. To current problems, advertising offers a series of familiar solutions: ever-developping knowledge, technical innovation, and scientific research.

19

GRAPHIC CREATIVITY

Some advertisers are known for their imaginative use of space. One interesting process consists in inundating your ad with small images, or empty images, or blackened ones, perhaps cut in half, as well as blank spaces, dotted lines, arrows, folded page-corners, a torn or crumpled sheet of paper.

You can also use special effects such as inversion or movement in your subject, images within images, three-dimensional effects, hazy focus, distortion, embossing, reflection and other luminous effects.

Many advertisers make their ads resemble newspaper articles, magazine covers, telephone yellow pages, classified ads, jigsaws puzzles, or paint-by-numbers pictures.

Others resort to original typographic characters and special words to inject originality into their ads. They will use exclamation marks or question marks, questions-and-answers, mathematical equations, parentheses, or onomatopoeia.

A final category of image resorts to the use of familiar objects. Visual clichés are used, such as tiny, everyday objects such as matches, an imitation postage-stamp, an envelope, a crossword puzzle, or a coupon.

This combination of two ads is typical of a process that consists in captivating the reader's attention by getting him to expect an answer. This tactic is known as "teasing". It lends a certain friendliness to your ad and helps to create a feeling of complicity with your reader, while of course holding his attention.

Three examples of images seeking to reproduce an abstract concept visually: reflection, escape, and power.

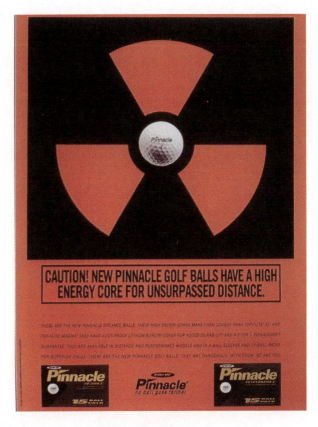

The transformed billboard has the advantage of attracting consumers' attention in a quick and powerful way. Its efficiency is immediate, and results are quickly felt.

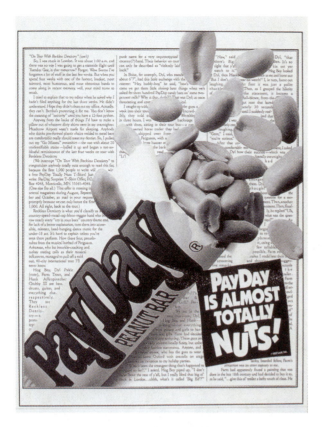

Some advertisers make their ads resemble newspaper articles or magazine covers.

20

THE HOUSE

No symbol better expresses private life and comfort than does the house. If you want to communicate the family ideal, showing the domestic dwelling is by far your best approach.

The window, complete with curtains, is a symbol of openness and receptivity. Small window-panes symbolize the cosiness of private life: one can peer through them, but the sense of touch is obstructed.

Inside the house, show the different rooms that constitute a family dwelling. Suggest mealtime by showing the kitchen, and show the bedroom with a bed and mirror.

Advertisers are fond of illustrating homes that contain a work space, with office and library, and a staircase.

On the second floor, one will invariably find a bedroom furnished with bed and mirror. This mirror is an important aspect of the house. Standing before it, one cannot cheat; albeit gently and naturally, it nonetheless returns us to ourselves and shows us ourselves as we are.

The bathroom's themes are not many. The main thing here is the tub, which you can use to express, in a fully narcissistic manner, all the sensual enjoyment of bath products. Of course, it is the product that must be shown at the center of this enjoyment.

Top:

The window, complete with curtains, is a symbol of receptivity. It is associated with the quality of openness. It suggests freedom, freshness, and well-being.

Bottom:

The door is where two worlds converge and flow into each other. It opens, and yet it contains mystery. The threshold is a place of transition.

The lock is associated with both opening and closing. To possess the key is to enjoy access to something or to someone.

The bathroom's themes are not numerous. The main elements: the tub and shower.

When you show a woman in her bath, express all the sensual and narcissistic pleasure of bath products. The woman of course must be enjoying these products.

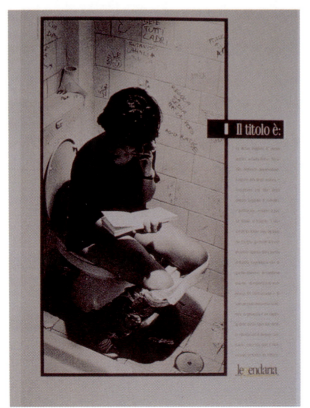

For a surprise effect, you may wish to refer directly to the bathroom as a place for bodily functions. In extreme cases, show a person seated on the toilet. Such an image is risky, but it will generate very high rates of attention.

21

INSTITUTIONAL CHARACTERS

You may find it useful to portray in your ads what are commonly called "institutional characters".

The institutional character is neither a star nor a mythical hero. Rather, he is an ordinary person, whose specificity as a character derives from his job or trade, or from his physical appearance, his behavior, or even the way he is dressed.

Institutional characters can permit you to reflect the different components that make up society. With these representative types, you can portray an age group, for example, or a gender or nationality. In fact, these characters are living clichés that help you position your product and identify your target clientele visually.

Each institutional character tells a tale that, over time, has become a stereotype. For example, the physician with his white smock and his stethoscope has become the very image of "scientific competence". The financier's place in advertising is symbolized by his wealth and his power. The cowboy incarnates freedom and manliness. And the detective tirelessly scrutinizes each clue looking for a lead.

See also: *woman* and *man*

To liven up your ads, surround your products with all sorts of characters whose status will be surmised from their dress and their physical appearance. Less famous than fictitious characters such as Ronald McDonald or the man from Glad, these cliché characters — a king, a detective, a chef from a famous restaurant — will help you to inject a human presence into your images and make them more original.

22

LEGENDARY CHARACTERS

Thanks to the imagination of advertisers, absolutely nothing is impossible! This is why advertising images often involve the use of characters from legends and fairy tales, with an atmosphere of mystery and magic.

But be mindful: in taking over references to legends and fairy tales, always limit yourself to the best-known characters. In this way, you will avoid confusing your readers with unfamiliar faces. With fantasy characters, you can tell a tale while at the same time opening up a world of meaningful symbols, evoking a memory, and perhaps a smile.

Pinocchio, the wooden puppet who became a boy, occupies an important place in the advertising world. Use him to reproach a tendency to lie, as symbolized by the long nose.

Recently, a US Army ad showed a knight, recognizable by his elaborate armor. This image immediately strikes a note of triumph and glory. As a warrior, the knight expresses an ideal. On his steed, with his shield and sword to protect him, he is a picture of courage.

See also: children

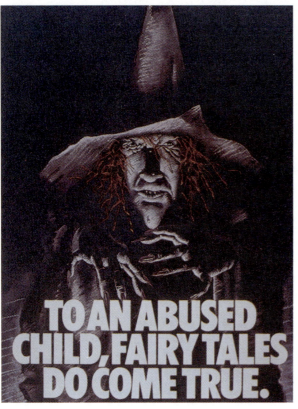

Top:

In fairy-tales, just as in the world of advertising, the prince often combines love with heroism. His ultimate reward is the undying love of the most beautiful girl in the land.

Bottom:

The witch, hideous and diabolical with her tall hat and her broom, is the antithesis of the ideal woman.

Cinderella is a hapless girl who ends up marrying a prince, thanks to a perfectly-fitting glass slipper. This character remains closely associated with shoes, brooms, mirrors, and pumpkins.

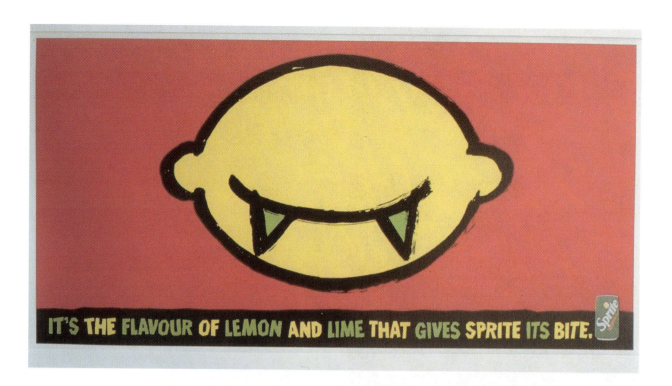

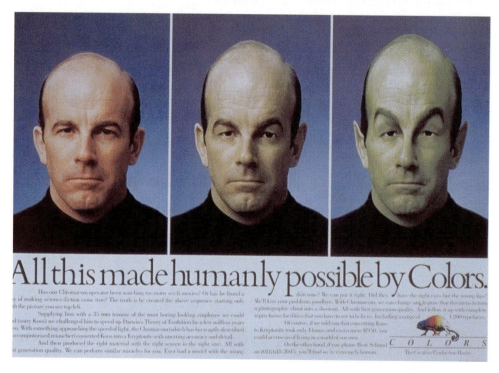

Should you decide to strike fear into the hearts of both young and old, you may choose from a series of frightening characters: Dracula, Frankeinstein, Martians, monsters, even robots.

23

LOVE

In your images, surprise consumers by associating your product with the tender ardor of love. In advertising, images of loving couples can even be a real necessity. The love can be either a lightning-bolt or an abiding passion. Your characters are young, they are strangers. They meet. After that, the world is no longer the same.

Heroism and overpowering emotion: every day, advertising reinvents myths and symbols that are in fact as old as the hills. If you want to turn your images into emotional power-houses, experiment with the posture of seduction. This can begin with certain emotionally charged objects: flowers, a heart, the moon, or gifts.

Visually, always try to give priority to theatrical qualities. This involves using meaningful and expressive gestures: the hand to the head or placed directly upon the buttocks, fingers enmeshed in the hair or placed upon the lips to reflect deep attachment. The embrace is yet another gesture-symbol. In the same vein, activities that require co-operation or the participation of the couple can constitute subtle (or even not-so-subtle) ways of representing the sensuality that readers adore.

At times, you may consider displaying rough or tumultuous activity between adults. In bouts of horse-play, objects such as pillows, streams of water, and beach-balls can be used as non-threatening projectiles.

See also: sexuality

When you want to give emotional punch to your images, be sure to make use of the gestures and body-language that are associated with seduction. Show the kiss on the lips, on the forehead, or on the neck.

Top:

The physical attitude most expressive of love is still the closeness of two bodies and, still more especially, the total embrace.

Bottom:

By presenting objects either intertwined or as somehow mysteriously attracted to each other, you can create images that possess the ability to astonish.

Top:

The lipstick trace — whether left upon the skin or on a shirt collar — is perhaps the most widely recognized symbol of love in advertising.

Bottom:

The hand touching the head, fingers enmeshed in the hair or placed upon the lips, these are signs of deep attachment. Two heads brought close together constitute the sign of an intimate bond between lovers.

Top:

Ads often use images of the body being supported in some way. As can be seen here, a young woman may be shown leaning on a man for support, holding on to him, or resting her head upon his shoulder.

Bottom:

Recently, images showing men being bolstered and encouraged by women have begun to appear. From an advertising point of view, these images constitute an important change and are well deserving of attention for that very reason. They seem increasingly likely to please a large portion of the female population. Keep it in mind.

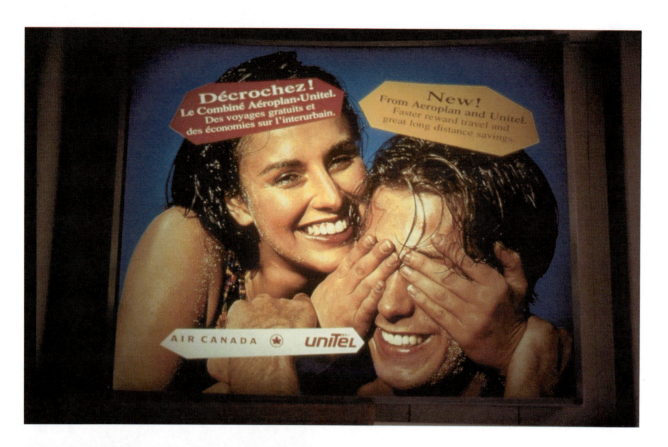

Top:

If you want to evoke the bliss of receiving a gift, show the "Guess what!" moment that comes just before its presentation.

Bottom:

"Wait while I catch you" could be the title of this playful situation, which regularly makes its way into advertising. Of course, these gestures are never intended to inflict injury: they are no more than eloquent signs of familiarity or intimacy.

When you want to evoke love, use a restaurant, a movie theater, or a beach.

These places seek not only to entice the reader. They also provide the action with necessary contextual elements. In this way, love becomes familiar and instantly recognizable: the rules are heeded, and your readers can easily identify with the characters in your ad.

Love and music are closely related. They suggest dancing and various other forms of physical contact.

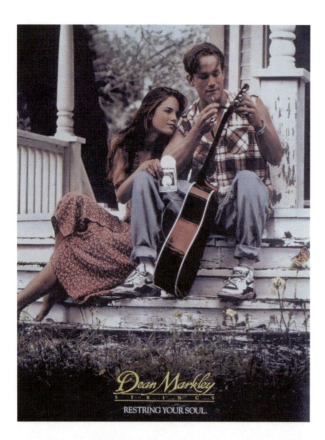

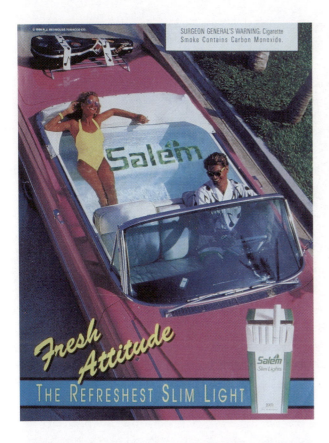

Advertising frequently resorts to the use of the convertible car. Although convertibles represent only two percent of annual car sales, they have nonetheless come to symbolize amorous encounters. According to the motivation studies expert Doctor Ernest Dichter, a man's convertible is symbolic of his mistress.

"The convertible symbolizes youth, freedom, and dreams", says Dichter. "Regular driving, on the other hand, is conservative and practical."

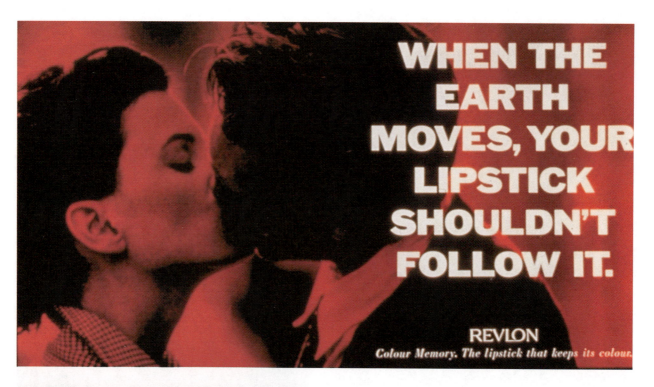

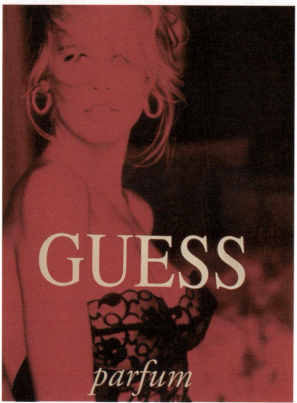

In advertising, each color has a specific emotional value. Red symbolizes love and warmth, sensuality and passion. It is the most dynamic color, with the greatest potential for action. Red increases blood pressure, muscular tension, and respiration. It is the color of eroticism.

Among all communications media, the telephone is the one most easily associated with intimate information. On the telephone, one can envision the ideal woman as a romantic and ever-attentive soul-mate.

The telephone provides intimacy at a distance.

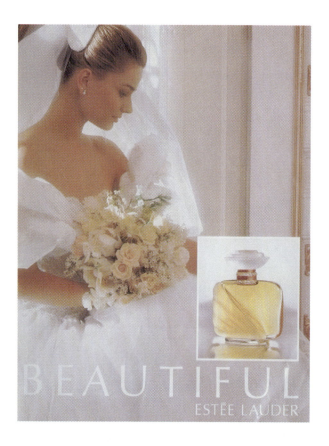

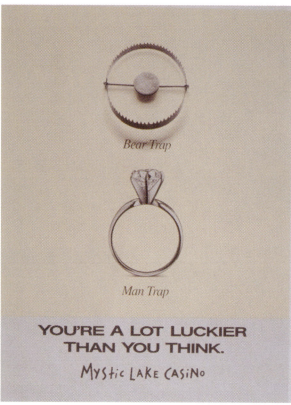

Top:

If you want to secure the attention of women, show pictures of weddings. Marriage celebrates the transition from celibacy to the family. It is a declaration of love. According to Starch, photographs of weddings are, along with those of babies and animals, the ones that catch the female reader's attention most effectively.

Bottom:

Wedding rings are seldom shown in advertising photography. Although the wedding ring is a highly symbolic object, it has practically disappeared from ad images. Its use has become flippant, even facetious.

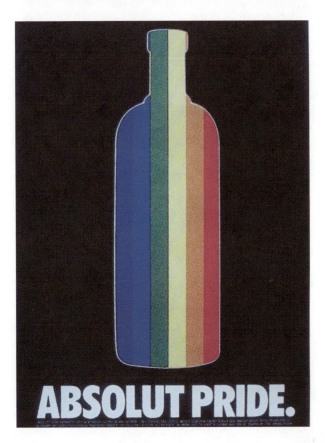

In advertising, the stable heterosexual couple is generally shown as the ideal. For a long time, it provided the sole model for the intimacy of love. Nevertheless, confronted with the reality of changing times, advertisers have begun to show homosexual relationships.

Early in the 1970s, the American agency responsible for the advertising budget of Gitane cigarettes began targeting the homosexual market. This campaign, showing the homosexual life-style and offering it a status-raising product, drove Gitane sales up by a full thirty percent. After that, the IKEA company, encouraged by Gitane's example, became the first enterprise to produce a televised commercial specifically aimed at homosexuals.

24

MAN

Advertisers often seem to repeat the same message: masculinity is virility, masculinity is strength. Men, as they appear in advertising, are tough guys. Suffused with the spirit of competition, they seem to value action over reflection.

A man's life, so the ads tell us, is one of adventure: war, the hunt, an ongoing struggle against the forces of nature. What counts here is this association of manliness with force, energy, and determination.

You can express virility with great conviction by showing men at work, on construction sites or in a forest setting, for example, but also by showing them engaged in both physical struggle and in sport. You can count on the efficacy of scenes depicting mountain climbers, boxers, auto racers, and seamen.

Similarly, do not hesitate to resort to images of "men-objects". Nowadays, the decorative male placed in sexually suggestive poses is unbeatable for attracting the attention of female readers.

Until recently, men were not particularly fashion-conscious. Fashion was a female preoccupation, so it was thought. But things change. If men in the early part of the twentieth century were attached to the overriding values of work and savings, today's men represent the culmination of several decades of preoccupation with appearances.

See: woman and sport

Pictures of activities requiring force and combativeness are essential for attracting men. In advertising, symbols of virility are very powerful, and images that express competition will invariably generate sales.

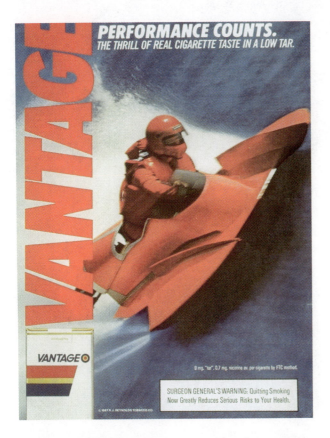

Top:

In order to suggest virility and competition, use images that evoke speed and power: formula-one racing cars, boats, planes, and motorbikes. Suggest risk and the presence of danger.

Bottom:

When your product is touted to men, athletics can be associated with boldness and adventure.

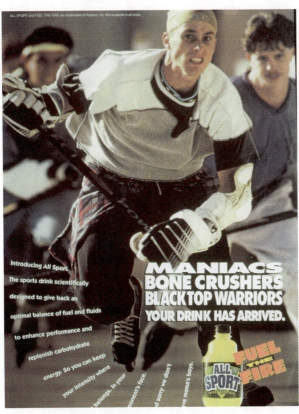

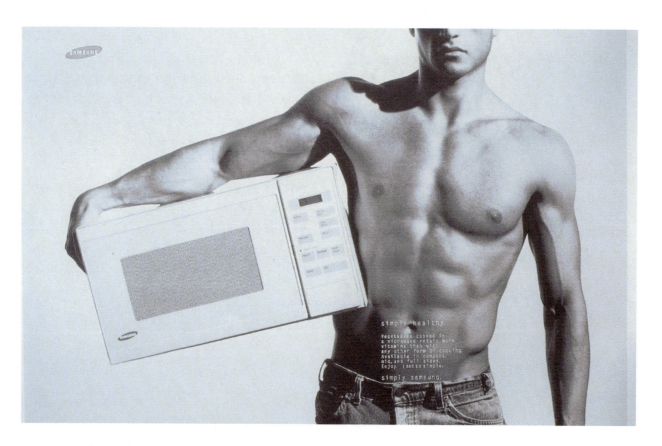

More than ever, it has become very profitable to insert a decorative male into your ads. He can have the look of an athlete, or be formally and elegantly dressed. Choose suggestive poses. The musculature of the back and biceps will both attract women's attention and invite identification by men.

25

THE PAST

To confirm your product's lasting value, use images that evoke the past, a time when our grandparents were young. In a word: the good old days.

For most people, images of the past arouse nostalgia. It is seen as a exquisite time, a kind of paradise. Indeed, we can all imagine a time when everyone was happier and life was easier.

Playing up the traditional aspect of a product often guarantees its profitability. The Jack Daniels firm, for example, has for decades been using black-and-white photography to evoke life's older traditions. Other advertisers prefer to place antiques in their images, thereby creating links with the past.

Occasionally, some advertisers, particularly in the technological field, will disparage the past, which to them is obsolete, a burden from which we should hasten to free ourselves.

Occasionally, the past can also provide an opportunity for bringing something up to date. In this way, the past can be made modern again. In fact, this is one way of creating shock images.

See: the future and outer space

Top

When you want to establish a serious tone, pictures of the past are a good idea. The past is invariably a source of nostalgia.

For many consumers, the mere fact that a product that has been in existence for years is reassuring. An established reputation is in itself a guarantee of quality in a world that is changing ever more rapidly.

Bottom

If you want to give your product an old-fashioned, well-established look, black-and-white photography can be a good idea. For decades, the Jack Daniels firm has been using black-and-white photography to evoke life's older traditions.

When you wish to call up fantasies of days gone by, be sure to insert meaningful and expressive objects into your images, objects such as the type-writer, the old-fashioned microphone, and the juke-box. These objects have an expressiveness that will successfully move the reader into the recent past.

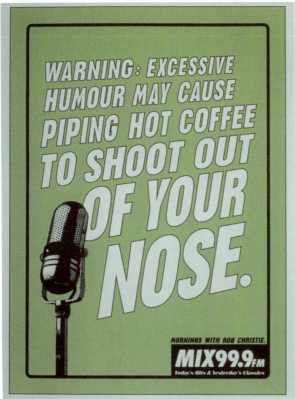

Some advertisers prefer to belittle the past, making it look old-fashioned and out of date. In this Coors ad, the past is only evoked in order to set off the positive side of modern life.

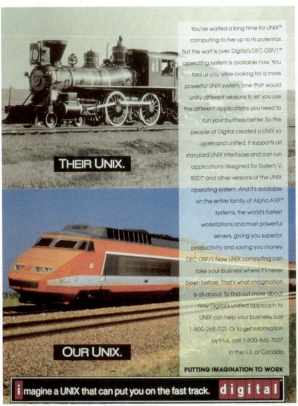

When you want to show how much things have changed for the better, your image can always contrast modern life with times past. Then only the present counts. The most powerful sign of the present is technology.

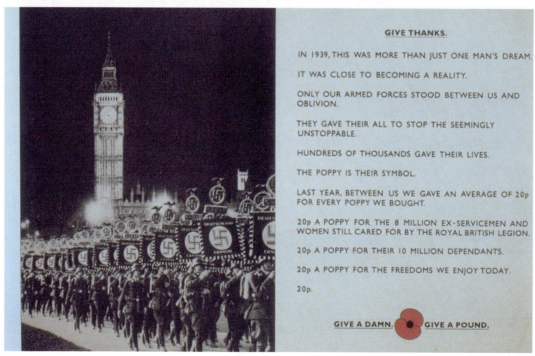

The past can also provide an opportunity for bringing something back into fashion. In this way, the past can be modernized. In fact, this is one way of creating shock images.

26

RELIGION

At first sight, one might well presume that there cannot be much connection between advertising and religion. And yet, many ads are brought into the purview of organized religion by the particular manner in which they borrow specific elements of liturgy and religious observance.

There are advertising images in which religion provides the general framework within which the ad's message is conveyed. At other times, this general religious inspiration tends to be more superficial.

Such religious ideas as the biblical account of creation are still very much alive in the world of advertising.

You can inspire religious nostalgia by using such symbols as the cross, the church, the stained-glass window, the bell, the monastery, and even the sky. Furthermore, you may wish to take advantage of associations with the compelling characters of the Bible by portraying Noah, Moses, Jesus, the angels, or Nativity characters.

The earthly paradise is easily symbolized by means of the snake, the vine-leaf, or the apple. Paradise is invariably a garden in spring, complete with gentle music, angels, birds, green rolling hills, and leafy trees.

In fact, it would seem that the languages of advertising and religion can often be brought quite effortlessly into harmonious rapport. However, I must advise you not to abuse people's devoutness, especially if your intention is to refer humorously to religious figures. Always remember that this kind of humor is very risky.

Advertising discourse is amply strewn with allusions to heaven, to hell, and to accounts of the flood.

At a time when religion is generally neglected, images of religious inspiration have paradoxically become more numerous than ever. Whether it is an image of Jesus, a halo, a nun, or the devil, these pictures have one thing in common: a mythical and primitive quality that startles and arouses the reader.

You can inspire religious nostalgia by the skillful use of holy symbols.

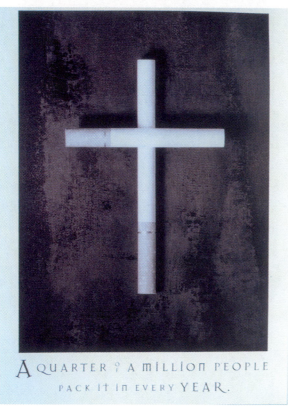

27

SEXUALITY

For attracting the attention of the consumer, sensuality and eroticism are frankly unbeatable. Do not hesitate to use various expressions of sexuality in order to invite your readers into a reverie where the only taboo is explicitness.

In your images, emphasize the seductive qualities of women and men. Show beautiful young women of generous proportions, legs raised or crossed, eyes closed or half-closed, and head thrown back. Exploit the suggestive power of self-contact. Use pictures of women with long legs, with hair pulled behind the ears, or hands on thighs.

Furthermore, do not hesitate to use the male sex-object. If in past times only the female body was used with a view towards embellishing the advertising message, today's ads freely use men for the same purposes. The muscular limbs of men are indeed an important factor of stimulation for women, and one simply cannot ignore that fact today.

No one should be shocked by the intensity and frankness with which sexual attraction is used in advertising. By definition, the ad image is meant to incite dreams. So if eroticism is part of the mix, it is because it corresponds so closely to the contemporary mind-set. It should also be pointed out that it was not advertising that invented eroticism.

Our culture is constantly making the erotic motive the primary ingredient and basic stimulus of daily life. This is what explains the near-automatic sexualization of everyday objects.

See also: love and the body

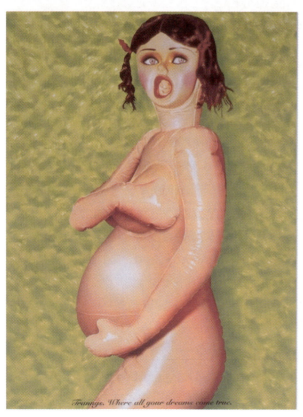

In their quest for new ways of representing sex, advertisers are always stretching the limits. This search sometimes takes on a particularly spectacular quality. At the end of the 20th century, pleasure is an obsession, and conventions are fading as never before. Identities are mixed and confounded in a world of false appearances and unforeseen realities. For example: a pregnant inflatable doll.

To be sure to capture your readers' attention, you can always show them beautiful young women.

When it first came out, this Calvin Klein ad (bottom right photograph) generated unparallelled attention levels throughout North America. Responding to in-depth interviews, readers confessed to having tried to identify bodies and to count the number of young girls in the ad; others sought rather to seek out the men.

There is, however, a problem here: studies indicate that when you use sex to attract attention, readers will pay attention to the photography and fail to retain the name of your product. So if you decide to use sex, insure that your media weight is sufficient to counterbalance this problem.

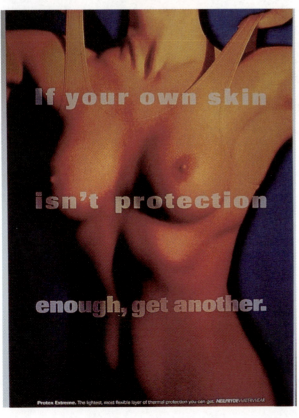

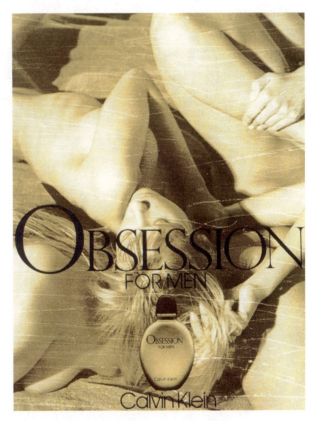

Some advertisers — especially in Europe — express sexual content with near-total nudity.

Exploit the suggestive power of self-contact. Hands pressed against thighs, chin, or shoulders have a very clear meaning: "Touch me!".

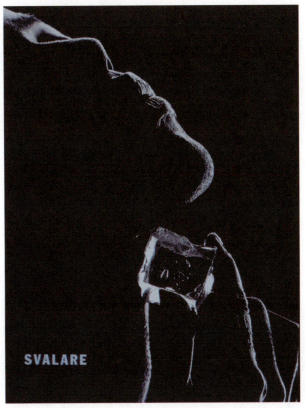

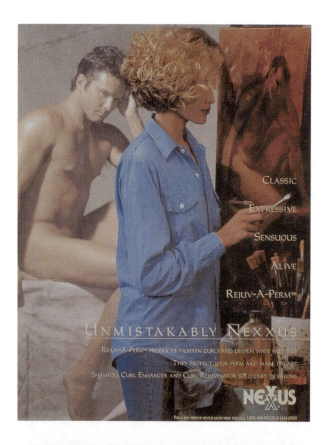

In traditional advertising strategies, sex is mainly defined as feminine: the challenge was to attract the masculine gaze, and feminine charms were nothing but a means for attaining this.

As a sign of the times, new fashion trends also exploit the bodies of men.

Nexus aims to appeal to women (upper left photograph) by showing a passive man in what is clearly a complete turnabout of the traditional situation. Henceforth, the woman is active, while the man poses.

28

SOCIAL PROBLEMS

Strangely enough, positive values are not the only ones to be found in advertising. Little by little, social problems such as pollution, violence, guns, and war have been finding their way into all kinds of ads. Poverty, malnutrition, drought, violence, and homelessness: the problems are many.

Some advertising images provide a general over-view of the great challenges with which society is faced. These ads would have been impossible to imagine ten years ago.

The growing drug problem has given rise to a series of key images: syringe, cocaine, pills, gaunt faces, and overriding visual drama. The suicide rate has been climbing in developed countries, and the scholastic drop-out rate is also on the rise.

The ad image also bears witness to the difficulties inherent in the defense of the environment. Since the 1980s, environmental concerns, such as those over the quality of the air and water, have been catching up with our anxieties over resource depletion.

These images are a sort of warning. They express an ecological consciousness.

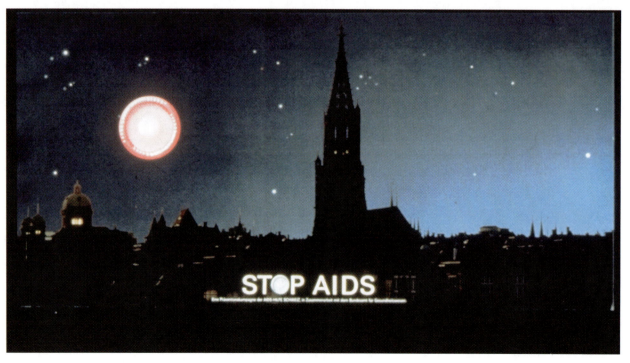

Pay close attention to AIDS. In the face of the AIDS epidemic, advertising has reacted with creativity, making the condom the media star of the hour.

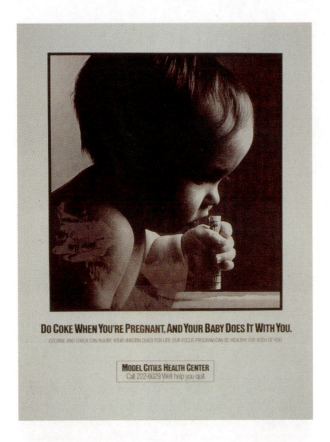

Advertising is all the more efficient when it is unexpected, especially when one is dealing with a subject as serious as that of illegal drugs.

These two messages are models. No other anti-drug campaign can boast of having used such forceful images. In ten years, social ad campaigns have changed completely. Long gone are the days of lengthy texts and tiny illustrations. Today, the textual content is wholly dominated by the visual.

If you intend to use your images to condemn environmental pollution, show smoky air, birds dying on banks and shores, garbage, and landfill sites.

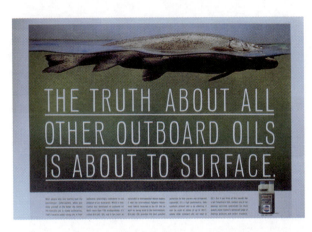

The anti-smoking campaign grows more strikingly original every day.

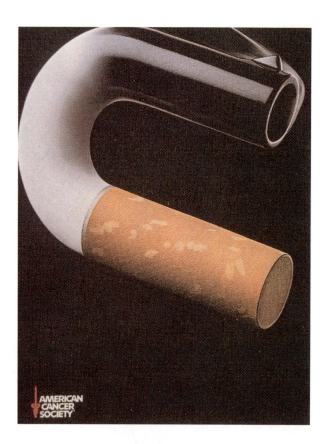

29

SPORT

Athletic activity is a symbol of good physical condition. Use it in images not only to promote an athletic event, but to sell beer, cigarettes, or cars as well.

If you wish to create sports pictures, be sure to insist on such factors as team spirit, physical exertion, and healthy vitality. Show couples and groups of friends jogging, swimming, or playing racquetball together. Let your images tap into the enthusiasm for physical well-being, which is in fact the physical equivalent of social success.

Celebrate performance by showing trendy activities like in-line skating. Show men and women conquering the elements with images of high altitude, waves, wind, or snow.

Use contact sports to show hard and intense physical effort. You will find these images of brute force to be extremely useful and profitable. The world of sport is a complex of key values: strength, determination, the desire to win, and hard training.

See also: woman and man

Athletic activities are depicted, first of all, by means of sporting equipment, such as tennis shoes, for example. Placed in various ways in the advertising image, these articles are extremely useful.

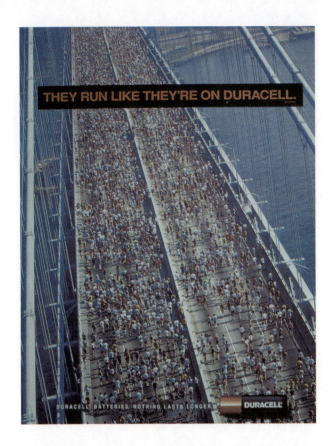

As often as possible, show vitality and physical exertion. Show men and women conquering the elements by means of images of high altitude, waves, wind, or snow.

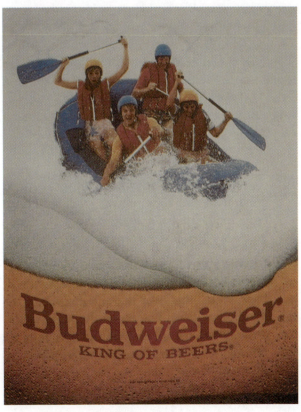

Sport has given rise to numerous visual metaphors that express strength, determination, and the will to win.

30

TIME

In advertising, time is of great value. It is a precious possession that we measure with precision. Time is the rhythm of life. Everywhere, the measure of time is indispensable to the ordering and functioning of society.

Nowadays, everyone is on the move. With the constant acceleration of progress, we are all living more rapidly than ever before. In fact, all mobility is seen as desirable, and the worst fate imaginable is to be "left behind".

Our institutions for the measure of time have given rise to such familiar scenes as the tardiness caused by highway detours and the seemingly interminable waiting in line. Time is also perceived as the regular succession of days and nights, of weeks, months, and years.

From one season to the next, warm and cold weather follow one upon the other. Advertising can very successfully express the notion of the annual cycle, eternal return, alternating seasons, and the springtime rebirth of nature.

Spring is evoked by the sight of swallows. Vegetation comes to life. Summer is synonymous with sun, holidays, and heat. Autumn is represented by rain and opening umbrellas, and the general atmosphere is a gloomy one. Leaves fall and the sky is grey. Winter is all snow and ice.

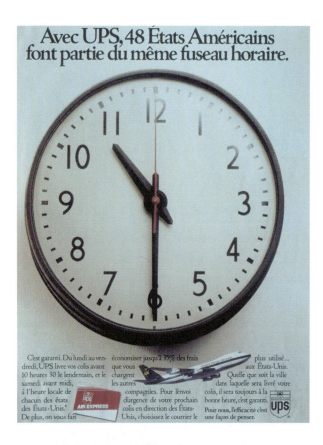

In the imaginary world of advertising, clocks and timepieces of all sorts abound. With the constant acceleration of progress, we are all living more rapidly than ever before.

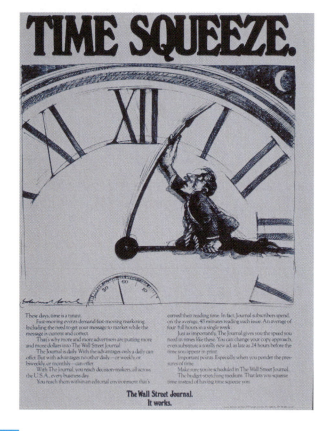

One very original way to show day and night consists in the use of an opacification process, such as the one made for the Yellow Pages. Special equipment is used to present different images according to whether it is day or night, since during the day the billboard receives natural sunlight, while at night, it is illuminated from behind.

Certain symbols give rise to very powerful images. An example: the shadow cast by a person or a product.

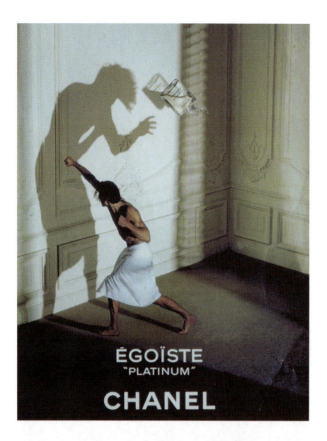

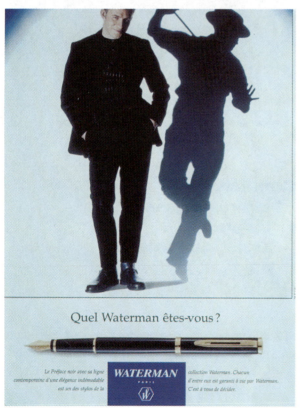

31

WEALTH

Wall Street, sunny beaches, yachts, ski-hills, swimming pools and palatial mansions: these are the images of advertising, and if we are to judge by the frequency with which they appear, consumers are obsessed by all that signifies luxury and social status.

When you want to suggest the influence of money and power, dress your models in exclusive collections. Use pictures of well-groomed gentlemen in stylish, immaculately polished shoes.

Although the range of colors that epitomize elegance and wealth is extensive, the tones that dominate are white, black, burgundy, green, and navy-blue, as well as combinations of white and black. Dark colors are generally preferred to light.

Successful people enjoy clubs and country homes. This is why ads so often depict rustic landscapes and the seaside, as well as stables, casinos, or castles, invariably surrounded with greenery and flowers.

Social symbolism has identified participation in certain sports as a symbol of membership in exclusive social circles. It is possible to evoke social status by depicting sports considered to be "aristocratic". Consumers of luxury products belong to a privileged class of people who are capable of underwriting the costs involved in the enjoyment of these expensive pass-times.

Never underestimate the symbolic importance of servants. With the decline in their numbers, such people as chauffeurs, porters, and even shoe polishers have acquired a distinctive social value.

See also: culture

Whether it is a white shirt, a dark suit, a tie or bow-tie, the up-scale garment possesses the advantage of suggesting wealth and good breeding. When you use these symbols, you bestow upon your image a measure of classical refinement.

Top:

Use symbols related to success in business, such as the red carpet.

Bottom:

Insist on the showing the kind of deep quality that only tradition can confer. Associate know-how and business efficiency with the early period of mechanization and the beginnings of industry. Show assembly-lines, industrial mechanisms, and gears.

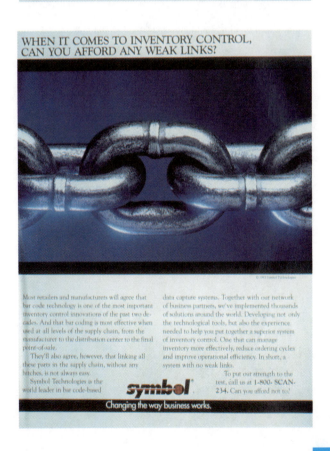

One's choice of mode of transportation says much about one's ambition and social success. The automobile, the plane, and the sailboat are unmistakable symbols of social exclusiveness.

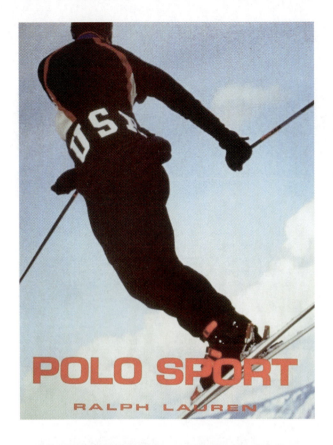

Social symbolism has identified participation in certain sports as a symbol of membership in exclusive social circles. It is possible to evoke social status by depicting sports considered to be "aristocratic". Consumers of luxury products belong to a privileged class of people who are capable of underwriting the costs involved in the enjoyment of these expensive pass-times.

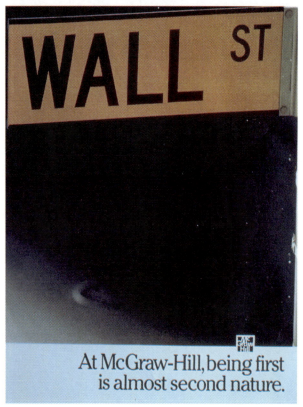

In a world where only the dollar counts, direct references to money and Wall Street are frequent.

Several symbols constitute implicit reminders of money, symbols such as the piggy-bank and the rising curve on a graph. In the proper context, a great many elements can take on new meaning. The ordinary bar-code is an excellent example of this.

In the bottom right image, the lines of the bar code form broken prison bars which hold up the words: "With Voor Merken, we work freely."

32

WOMAN

Over the years, advertising has built up an image of women that admits of no more than the most minor variations of detail.

One model for the acceptable representation of the woman is based upon traditional values. A woman's life, according to this model, is situated between the poles of feminine passivity and romantic availability.

A second model uses symbols that seem to emerge from a new set of feminine values, values that are becoming ever more deeply rooted in the life of our society. Typical of this model would be pictures of female athletes or of women that play important social roles.

Given the changing circumstances, it is essential that your advertising images reflect this important trend. If you should work with models over the age of thirty, then they must incarnate the image of the career woman climbing the social hierarchy.

At the same time, you may offer images inspired by the model of femininity that we are accustomed to seeing in the fashion pages. In others words, admit and give expression to the new cultural model, but be sure to maintain the woman's natural attributes, such as beauty and maternity.

Actually, this seeming contradiction is not really altogether surprising. Advertising, by reason of its very objectives, is compelled to become one with the socio-cultural context of its target audience. To be seen, your ad will have to reply to public tastes. Otherwise, its destiny will be to remain invisible.

See: man, the body, sexuality, and love

A good many advertising images choose to place women in a long-established role: the nude, or the sexy and suggestively posed woman. Although images showing young women in suggestive poses invariably secure high rates of attention, it is not necessarily always a good idea to attract men's notice by associating brand names with erotic images. Indeed, research has shown that brands advertised with suggestions of eroticism are ultimately less well remembered than are those brands that are advertised with more neutral illustrations.

For some years now, the world of advertising has been transforming its representation of women.

The immediate consequence of this new trend has been the fact that advertising no longer necessarily presents a woman as wife or mother. Women today are administrators in large firms. They are professional, businesslike, and increasingly unconventional.

In fact, the woman that one most often sees in advertising today is determined and assertive.

Personal qualities traditionally associated with men are now attributed to women: today, women in ads will flirt, part their legs, smoke cigars, and generally adopt an imposing demeanor.

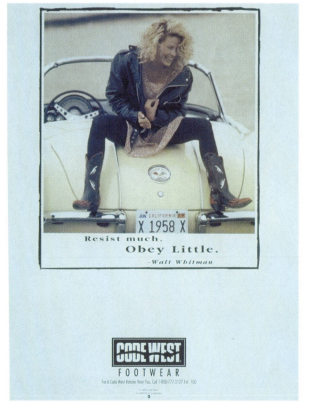

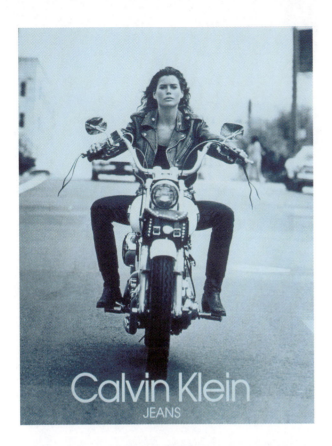

When you put modern women into your images, make ample use of the themes of physical effort and success. Consider for example: women developping their muscles by working out with weights, women climbing mountains, lacing up boxing-gloves, driving motorbikes, playing ice-hockey or soccer. By showing women of determined character, you can build up an image of sexual equality.

33

YOUNG PEOPLE

In advertising, youth is synonymous with adventure and enthusiasm. Above all, youth is a time of life characterized by freedom. Rules, one might say, are ruled out.

In your ad images, help your young readers to recognize themselves by dressing your models in a relaxed, informal way. Put them into jeans and leather jackets, while avoiding the traditional jacket and tie.

Images of nonconformity are always a good bet. Show young people eager to develop their own personalities, and show how this desire brings them into conflict with the society that surrounds them.

The young adult is often a student. Show this status by dressing him in an academic gown. This same garb can be used to impart an academic ambience to many other situations.

Although youth is also characterized by an emerging sexual consciousness and experience, the dominant value nevertheless remains friendship. If you consider the entire range of advertising images portraying young adults, you will immediately notice the unifying theme of friendship.

See also: love and the body

Young adults are very responsive to life-style themes in advertising. If you want to get their attention, rely on such themes as music, friendship, freedom, and nonconformity.

CONCLUSION

If you want your ads to succeed in today's busy marketplace, you cannot avoid giving priority to the visual medium. The best way to penetrate consumers' resistance is to simplify your concept and to use images that deliver your message in mere fractions of a second.

Your images must communicate some characteristic quality of your product and invite consumers to purchase your brand for emotional, rather than rational, reasons.

In order to work well, your ad has got to make a visual proposition sufficiently interesting to consumers to stir them up, get them excited. If you limit your message to the listing of advantages born of minimal technical differences, your ad will be lifeless and ineffective. On the other hand, if you use emotionally loaded images, you will immeasurably increase your odds of winning your reader's attention.

The triumph of television, movies, and photography has ultimately imposed a dominant principle on advertising: everything yields to emotion and the image.

Advertising — as all persuasive communication — is a primitive sort of communication. It is not to be confused with an exercise of highly complex reasoning.

BIBLIOGRAPHY

Atwan, Robert. *Edsels, Luckies and Frigidaires: Advertising the American Way*, New York, Dell Publishing Co., 1979.

Baker, Stephen. *Visual Persuasion: The Effects of Pictures on the Subconscious*, New York, McGraw-Hill, 1961.

Barthes, Roland. *Mythologies*, London, Paladin, 1973.

Bogart, Leo. *Strategy in Advertising*, Chicago, Crain Books, 1984.

Boorstin, Daniel. *The Image*, New York, Atheneum, 1962.

Burton, Philip Ward, and Scott Purvis. *Which Ad Pulled Best?* Lincolnwood, NTC Business Books, 1987.

Caples, John. *Tested Advertising Methods*, Englewood Cliffs, Prentice-Hall, 1987.

Cheskin, Louis. *Why People Buy*, New York, Liveright Publishing Corporation, 1959.

Cossette, Claude. *Les Images démaquillées*, Québec, Les Éditions Riguil Internationales, 1985.

Debord, Guy. *Society of the Spectacle*, Detroit, Black and Red, 1970.

Dichter, Ernest. *The Strategy of Desire*, Garden City, New York, Doubleday & Company, 1960.

Dobrow, Larry. *When Advertising Tried Harder*, New York, Friendly Press, 1984.

Goffman, Erving. *Gender Advertisements*, New York, Harper & Row, 1979.

Goodrum, Charles and Helen Dalrymple. *Advertising in America: The First 200 Years*, New York, Harry N. Abrams, 1990.

Goldman, Robert and Stephen Papson. *Sign Wars: The Cluttered Landscape of Advertising*, New York, The Guilford Press, 1995.

Leiss, William, Stephen Kline, and Sut Jhally. *Social Communication in Advertising*, New York, Methuen, 1986.

Leymore, Varda. *Hidden Myth: Structure and Symbolism in Advertising*, London, Heinemann, 1975.

Marchand, Roland. *Advertising in the American Dream: Making Way for Modernity 1920-1940*, Berkeley, University of California Press, 1985.

Martineau, Pierre. *Motivation in Advertising*, New York, Mc Graw-Hill, 1957.

Messaris, P. *Visual Persuasion: the Role of Images in Advertising*, Thousand Oaks, Sage, 1997.

Randazzo, Sal. *Mythmaking on Madison Avenue: How Advertisers Apply the Power of Myth & Symbolism to Create Leadership Brands*, Chicago, Probus, 1993.

Schudson, Michael. *Advertising, the Uneasy Persuasion: Its Dubious Impact on American Society*, New York, Basic Books, 1984.

Starch, Daniel. *Measuring Advertising Readership and Results*, New York, McGraw-Hill, 1966.

Twitchell, James B. *Adcult USA*, New York, Columbia, 1995.

Williamson, Judith. *Decoding Advertisements*, London, Marion Boyards, 1978.

OTHER TITLES BY LUC DUPONT

1001 Advertising Tips (ISBN: 0-9699834-0-9)
Written in how-to terms, this book is a step-by-step guide to create advertising that sells.

Using dozens of examples of advertising campaigns and marketing strategies, it offers you the insight, tools and techniques to market any product or service.

- The importance of positioning your product or service
- Seventy-two key words in advertising
- Color: what it can do for you
- How to write successful headlines and copy
- What kind of slogans are the most effective
- Using layout and typeface to generate business
- Maximizing your results with repetition
- Creating high-impact illustrations
- The impact of zapping on TV ads
- Eleven ways to make your advertising more credible
- Contests & sweepstakes: pros and cons
- The power of corporate and brand logos
- When to use testimonials and endorsements
- Comparative advertising: when to use it
- Choosing a product name
- Pricing: a powerful weapon
- Using promotion and sponsorship, and much more!

You will also find a collection of the most effective ads dominating the market in the past ten years. An extensive index and chapter notes are provided for easy referencing. ($19.95US; $28.95CAN)